Orby Shipley

Eucharistic Litanies from ancient sources

Orby Shipley

Eucharistic Litanies from ancient sources

ISBN/EAN: 9783742837998

Manufactured in Europe, USA, Canada, Australia, Japa

Cover: Foto ©Andreas Hilbeck / pixelio.de

Manufactured and distributed by brebook publishing software (www.brebook.com)

Orby Shipley

Eucharistic Litanies from ancient sources

Eucharistic
LITANIES:

FROM

Ancient Sources.

BY

THE REV. ORBY SHIPLEY, M.A.

London:
JOSEPH MASTERS, ALDERSGATE STREET,
AND NEW BOND STREET.
M.DCCC.LX.

LONDON:
PRINTED BY JOSEPH MASTERS AND CO.,
ALDERSGATE STREET.

PREFACE.

As the contents of the following pages pretend to no originality, beyond the selection of the materials, it seems needless to particularise, further than the Title Page, & the Table of Contents disclose them, the sources from which, in each particular case, the Litanies are derived. Many of the Litanies have previously appeared in print, either in their present shape, or under different combinations. Mr. Bright's "Ancient Collects;" Mr. Malan's "Prayers for the Holy Communion" from Eastern Sources; "Holy Communion," published by Mr. Lumley; "The Eucharistic Month," translated by Mr. G. Cosby White; "A Companion to Holy Communion," by a Layman; Mr. Parker's Edition of "The Imitation of CHRIST;" & other works, have, with much generosity, been placed at the Editor's disposal, in order

order that the present collection may be the more complete. The materials from these storehouses of Devotional Treasures have been used in two ways. They have been extracted entire, as they were published, as Litanies: & they have been borrowed piece-meal, & afterwards arranged as they now appear. By the former plan, most of the more beautiful of the Litanies in our language, have been collected; & by the latter, most of the more valued & many of the more familiar passages of those devotions we commonly employ, have been reproduced, in a single Volume.

In addition to Litanies from these sources, others have been contributed, from Holy Scripture, Ancient Liturgies, or other Manuals, by friends who have intrusted them, on their first publication, or otherwise, to the present Collection.

It will thus appear, that this Compilation—which contains Litanies on the Most Holy Communion, drawn from Eucharistic Sources, or founded upon Eucharistic Truths,—owes its origin, to a very large extent, either to the indirect assistance, or to the active co-operation of numerous kind friends, to whom the Editor is much indebted.

A Se-

A Second Part, in the event of its publication, will contain *Penitential Litanies, & those of a more subjective character than are to be found in the present Volume.* Amongst others, it is proposed to publish Litanies on the Adorable Passion of our Blessed LORD, in the very words of Holy Scripture; on the Words of CHRIST, & of the enemies of CHRIST; for the Sick, for the Dying, & for those whom " not lost, but gone before," the dictates of natural instinct, no less than the custom of CHRIST'S Church Catholic, bids us remember in our prayers—the Faithful Departed; for the Seasons of Lent, & Advent; &—which are altogether omitted in the First Part—Litanies of GOD, the HOLY GHOST.

For the arrangement of the Litanies, the Editor is alone responsible. In many of them, where it is practicable, it has been endeavoured, after the example of Bishop Andrewes, & other former Devotions, to accommodate the form to the sense, & to assist the higher faculties by means of the lower. For convenience' sake, a selection of " Invocations" & " Conclusions" respectively commence, & close the Volume. This leaves the subject matter of the

the Litany free from either adjunct. A little consideration will show how the Litany is to be said. The introductory words, containing the Titles of the Divine PERSON addressed, may be repeated before each succeeding Invocation. The Form, "That it may please Thee," &c., may also, in many cases, be supplied where it is needed. And the Response may always be repeated in full, even where, for the sake of marking more strongly the divisions of the several Petitions, the first words alone are printed.

May Almighty GOD be pleased to bless the publication of this little Book to His greater Glory.

ORBY SHIPLEY.

Epiphany Tide,
 A.D. 1860.

CONTENTS.

	PAGE
INVOCATIONS	1

LITANIES OF GOD, THE FATHER;
 j. From the Collects in the Book of Common Prayer   9
 ij. From the fame 17
 iij. From the Secretæ, &c., of the Gallican Miffal   26

LITANIES OF GOD, THE SON;
 j. From the Collects & Prayers of the Paris Miffal   37
 ij. From the Mozarabic Liturgy of S. Ifidore . 49
 iij. From the Euchariftic Month . . . 60
 iv. From the Hours & Miffal of the Sarum Ufe . 72
 v. From the Devotions of S. Ambrofe, &c. . 85
 vj. From S. Paul's Epiftle to the Hebrews . . 92
 vij. From the fame 99
 viij. From a Copto-Arabic MS. 105
 ix. From the Armenian 110
               x. From

CONTENTS.

		PAGE
x.	From an Ethiopic MS.	114
xj.	From a Litany of the Tenth Century	117
xij.	From the Sacramentary of S. Gregory	120
xiij.	From the same	126
xiv.	From the Imitation of CHRIST, Book iv	135
xv.	From an Ancient Litany	141
xvj.	From the Paradise of the Christian Soul	147
xvij.	From early English Sources	153
xviij.	From an old Litany of German origin	157

CONCLUSIONS 166

INVOCATIONS.

O GOD, the FATHER, of Heaven;
O GOD, the SON, Redeemer of the world;
O GOD, the HOLY GHOST, Proceeding from the
FATHER & the SON;
O Holy, Bleſſed, & Glorious TRINITY, Three
Perſons, & One GOD;
Have mercy upon us, miſerable ſinners.

O GOD, the FATHER,
Make ſpeed to ſave us;
O GOD, the SON,
Make ſpeed to ſave us;
O GOD, the COMFORTER,
Make ſpeed to ſave us;
O GOD, the HOLY TRINITY,
Make ſpeed to ſave us;
O LORD, *make haſte to help us.*

INVOCATIONS.

GOD, the FATHER; GOD, the SON;
GOD, the HOLY GHOST;
Save, & protect us,
Now, & for evermore. Amen.

In the Name
Of the FATHER, of the SON,
& of the HOLY GHOST;
Amen.

Everlasting FATHER,
From Whom are all things;
Eternal SON,
Through Whom are all things;
HOLY SPIRIT,
In Whom are all things;
Blessed TRINITY,
Holy, & Undivided;
Be favourable,
Spare us, good LORD.

LORD, have mercy.
CHRIST, *have mercy.*
LORD, have mercy.

GOD, the FATHER; *Spare us.*
GOD,

INVOCATIONS. 3

GOD, the SON ; *Save us.*
GOD, the SPIRIT ; *Sanctify us.*

Holy FATHER ; *Be merciful.*
Only SON ; *Be favourable.*
Blessed SPIRIT ; *Be gracious.*

O GOD, the FATHER,
Accepter of the Sacrifice ;
O GOD, the SON,
Priest, and Victim in the Sacrifice ;
O GOD, the SPIRIT,
Consecrator of the Sacrifice ;
Save us, & help us,
We humbly beseech Thee, O LORD.

O CHRIST, hear us ;
O CHRIST, *graciously hear us.*

The Power of the FATHER ; *guide us.*
The Wisdom of the SON ; *enlighten us.*
The Working of the SPIRIT ; *quicken us.*

O Thou, Who didst create ;
Destroy not us whom Thou hast created.
O Thou,

O Thou, Who didst redeem;
Destroy not us whom Thou hast redeemed.

O Thou, Who didst regenerate;
Destroy not us whom Thou hast regenerated.

KYRIE, Eleison.
CHRISTE, Eleison.
KYRIE, Eleison.

O GOD, the FATHER,
Who created us, & all the world;
O GOD, the SON,
Who redeemed us, & all mankind;
O GOD, the HOLY GHOST,
Who sanctifieth us, & all the Elect;
Be propitious.

FATHER,
Whose Blessed SON was baptized;
WORD,
Into Whose Death we are baptized;
PARACLETE,
By Whom the waters of Baptism are sanctified;
THREE in ONE, & ONE in THREE,
In Whose Name we are baptized;

Suffer

INVOCATIONS.

*Suffer us to come unto Thee,
& forbid us not.*

FATHER of Mercy;
SAVIOUR of sinners;
Life-giving SPIRIT;
Spare us, Good LORD.

CREATOR of the Light;
SHEPHERD of the Sheep;
Thrice Holy SPIRIT;
Ever Blessed TRINITY;

O GOD, the Joy of Saints;
O GOD, the Reward of Saints;
O GOD, the Sanctifier of Saints;

O FATHER Almighty,
Who hast prepared for us
The Safe Harbour of Thy Holy Church;
O CHRIST, our King,
Who hast given unto us
Thy Holy & Vivifying BODY & BLOOD;
O True SPIRIT,
Who hast renewed Thy Holy Church;
Alleluia.

O GOD,

INVOCATIONS.

O GOD, the FATHER of Mercies;
O GOD, the Mediator between GOD & Man;
O GOD, the Enlightener of hearts;
O GOD, the Undivided TRINITY;

By the tender Yearnings of the FATHER;
By the Bloody Wounds of the SON;
By the unutterable Plaints of the SPIRIT;
Give ear, O LORD, have mercy, O LORD,
O LORD, hearken, & do.

O Creator of the world;
O Redeemer of mankind;
O Perfecter of the elect;
O Sacred TRINITY;
Be clement.

PART

PART I.

EUCHARISTIC LITANIES.

LITANIES OF GOD THE FATHER.

[*In Preparation for Holy Communion.*][1]

I.

Most gracious GOD,
Who dost govern all things
In Heaven & Earth;
Graciously hear us, Good LORD.

Who knowest us to be set in the midst
Of so many, & great dangers,
That we cannot always stand upright;
Graciously.

Who seest that we put not our trust
In any thing that we do;
Graciously.

---

[1] *From the Collects in the Book of Common Prayer.*

Who haſt taught us
That all our doings, without Charity,
Are nothing worth ;
Graciouſly.

Who hateſt nothing that Thou haſt made,
& doſt forgive the ſins of all that are penitent ;
Graciouſly.

Who ſeeſt that we have no power
Of ourſelves, to help ourſelves ;
Graciouſly.

Who ſhoweſt to them that be in error
The Light of Thy Truth,
That they may return to the way of Godlineſs ;
Graciouſly.

Who alone canſt order
The unruly wills,
& affections of ſinful men ;
Graciouſly.

We ſinners,
Do beſeech Thee,

That we may both perceive, & know
What

OF GOD THE FATHER.

What things we ought to do;
& alfo, may have Grace, & Power
Faithfully to fulfil the fame;
Hear, & fave.

That Thou grant us fuch ftrength, & protection,
As may fupport us in all dangers,
& carry us through all temptations;
Hear, & fave.

That we, who lean only upon the hope
Of Thy Heavenly Grace,
May evermore be defended
By Thy mighty Power;
Hear, & fave.

That Thou pour into our hearts,
That moft excellent Gift of Charity;
Hear, & fave.

That we, worthily lamenting our fins,
& acknowledging our wretchednefs,
May obtain remiffion, & forgivenefs;
Hear, & fave.

That we may be defended
From all adverfities

Which

Which may happen to the body;
& from all evil thoughts,
Which may assault & hurt the soul;
Hear, & save.

That we may eschew those things
That are contrary to our Profession;
& may follow all such things
As are agreeable to the same;
Hear, & save.

That we may love the thing
Which Thou commandest,
& may desire
That which Thou dost promise;
Hear, & save.

II.

Most Gracious GOD,
Who art the Strength
Of all that put their trust in Thee,
Graciously hear us, Good LORD.

Who never failest to help, & govern
Them whom Thou dost bring up

In

OF GOD THE FATHER.

In Thy stedfast Fear, & Love;
Graciously.

Without Whom,
Nothing is strong, nothing is holy;
Graciously.

Who hast prepared for them that love Thee,
Such good things as pass man's understanding;
Graciously.

Who art the Author, & Giver
Of all good things;
Graciously.

Whose never-failing Providence
Ordereth all things in Heaven & earth;
Graciously.

Who declarest Thy Almighty Power
Most chiefly in showing
Mercy, & Pity;
Graciously.

Who art always more ready to hear,
Than we to pray;
& art wont to give more
Than either we desire, or deserve;
Graciously.

Of Whose only Gift it cometh
That Thy faithful People do unto Thee,
True & laudable Service;
Graciously.

Our Refuge, & Strength,
Who art the Author of all Godliness;
Graciously.

We sinners,
Do beseech Thee.

That those things we ask faithfully,
We may obtain effectually;
Hear, & save.

That we may so faithfully serve Thee
In this life,
That we fail not, finally, to attain
Thy Heavenly Promises;
Hear, & save.

That Thou mayest forgive us those things
Whereof our conscience is afraid;
& mayest give us those good things
Which we are not worthy to ask;
Hear, & save.

That,

OF GOD THE FATHER.

That, running the way of Thy Commandments,
We may obtain Thy Promises;
& be made partakers of
Thy Heavenly Treasures;
Hear, & save.

That Thou put away from us
All hurtful things;
& give us those things
Which be profitable for us;
Hear, & save.

That we may obtain Thy Promises,
Which exceed all we can desire;
Hear, & save.

That we may so pass through
Things temporal,
That we finally lose not the
Things Eternal;
Hear, & save.

That we may obtain
That which Thou dost promise,
Make us to love
That which Thou dost command;
Hear, & save.

That

That in keeping of Thy Commandments
We may pleafe Thee both in will & deed ;
Hear, & fave.

That Thou increafe in us true Religion,
Nourifh us with all Goodnefs,
& of Thy great Mercy
Keep us in the fame ;
Hear, & fave.

That we, who cannot do anything
That is good without Thee,
May by Thee, be enabled to live
According to Thy Will ;
Hear, & fave.

LITANIES OF GOD THE FATHER ALMIGHTY.

[*On the Life of our Blessed LORD.*]¹

I.

Almighty GOD,
Who didst announce the Incarnation
Of Thy SON JESUS CHRIST,
By the message of an Angel;
Be merciful.

Give us Grace that we may cast away
The works of darkness,
& put upon us the armour of Light,
Now in the time of this mortal life,
In which Thy Blessed SON
Came to visit us, in great humility; &
Be merciful.

---

¹ *From the Collects in the Prayer Book.*

Whose Only Son, Jesus Christ,
At His first coming,
Did send His Messenger
To prepare His Way before Him;
Be merciful.

Who hast given Thy Only Begotten Son
To take our Nature upon Him,
& to be born of a Pure Virgin;
Be merciful.

Who madest Thy Blessed Son
To be circumcised,
& obedient to the Law, for man;
Be merciful.

Whose Only Begotten Son
Was presented in the Temple,
In substance of our Flesh;
Be merciful.

Who, by the leading of a Star,
Didst manifest Thine Only Son
To the Gentiles;
Be merciful.

Whose Blessed Son was manifested,
That He might destroy the works of the devil,
& make

& make us the Sons of GOD,
& heirs of eternal Life;
Be merciful.
We sinners,
Beseech Thee,
That, having this Hope,
We may purify ourselves, as He is Pure;
That when He shall appear again,
With Power, and great Glory,
We may be made like unto Him,
In His eternal and glorious Kingdom;
Vouchsafe to hear us.

That we may perceive, & know
What things we ought to do;
& also may have Grace, & Power,
Faithfully to fulfil the same;
Vouchsafe.

That we may be presented unto Thee,
With pure, and clean hearts;
Vouchsafe.

That, our hearts, and all our members,
Being mortified from worldly and carnal lusts,
We may in all things obey
Thy

Thy Blessed Will;
Vouchsafe.

That, being regenerate & made Thy children,
By Adoption, & Grace,
We may daily be renewed by Thy HOLY SPIRIT;
Vouchsafe.

That the Ministers & Stewards
Of Thy Mysteries,
May so prepare and make ready His Way,
By turning the hearts of the disobedient
To the Wisdom of the Just;
That at His Second Coming to Judge the World,
We may be found
An acceptable people in Thy Sight;
Vouchsafe.

That, by His Cross, & Passion,
We may be brought
Unto the Glory of His Resurrection;
Vouchsafe.

II.

Almighty GOD,
Whose Blessed SON, for our sake

Did

Did fast forty days & forty nights;
Be merciful.

Who, of Thy tender Love towards mankind,
Hast sent Thy SON, our SAVIOUR,
To take upon Him our Flesh,
& to suffer death upon the Cross,
That all should follow the example of
His great Humility;
Be merciful.

Whose Only SON, our LORD JESUS CHRIST,
Was contented to be betrayed;
& given up into the hands of wicked men;
& to suffer death upon the Cross;
Be merciful.

By Whose SPIRIT
The whole Body of the Church
Is governed, & sanctified;
Be merciful.

Who hast made all men,
& hatest nothing that Thou hast made;
Nor wouldest the death of a sinner,
But rather, that he should be converted & live;
Be merciful.

Into

Into the death of Whose Blessed Son
We are baptized;
& with Whose Son we are buried,
By mortifying our corrupt affections;
Be merciful.

Who, through Thy Only Begotten Son,
Hast overcome death,
& opened unto us the gate of everlasting Life;
Be merciful.

Who hast given Thy Son, Jesus Christ,
To die for our Sins,
& to rise again for our Justification;
Be merciful.

Who hast given Thy Blessed Son
To be unto us, both a Sacrifice for sin;
& also, an Ensample of Godly life;
Be merciful.

Whose Son, our Lord Jesus Christ,
Ascended up into the Heavens;
Be merciful.

Who hast exalted Thine Only Son,
With great triumph,

Unto

Unto Thy Kingdom in Heaven;
Be merciful.

Who didst teach the hearts
Of Thy faithful people,
By the sending to them the Light
Of Thy HOLY SPIRIT;
Be merciful.

We sinners,
Beseech Thee,

That, by Thy HOLY SPIRIT,
We may have a right judgment in all things;
& evermore rejoice
In His Holy Comfort;
Vouchsafe to hear us.

That Thou send Thine HOLY GHOST
To comfort us;
& to exalt us to the same Place,
Whither our SAVIOUR CHRIST is gone before;
Vouchsafe.

That, in heart and mind, we may ascend;
& with Him continually dwell;
Vouchsafe.

That we may thankfully receive
His ineſtimable Benefit;
& alſo, may daily endeavour, ourſelves
To follow the Bleſſed Steps
Of His Moſt Holy Life;
Vouchſafe.

That we may ſo put away the leaven
Of malice & wickedneſs,
That we may always ſerve Thee in pureneſs
Of living and truth;
Vouchſafe.

That, as Thou doſt put into our minds
Good deſires;
So, by Thy continual Help,
We may bring the ſame to good effect;
Vouchſafe.

That, through the grave & gate of death,
We may paſs to our joyful Reſurrection;
Vouchſafe.

That all Jews, Turks, Infidels, & Heretics,
May be ſaved
Among the remnant of true Iſraelites,
& be

& be made one Fold under One Shepherd;
Vouchsafe.

That every member of the Church
In his vocation, & ministry,
May truly & Godly serve Thee;
Vouchsafe.

That we may both follow the example of
His Patience,
& also be made partakers of
His Resurrection;
Vouchsafe.

That we may use such abstinence,
That the flesh being subdued to the Spirit,
We may ever obey Thy Godly Motions,
In Righteousness, & true Holiness;
Vouchsafe.

LITANIES OF THE ETERNAL FATHER.

[On the Life of His Blessed SON.][1]

I.

O LORD, our Heavenly FATHER,
Look upon the afflictions of Thy people,
& send to us our Mighty Deliverer
From Heaven; &
Spare us, Good LORD.

Who hast founded the Salvation of the world,
On the Incarnation of Thy Word;
Spare us.

Whose Co-eternal SON
Was conceived, for the Salvation of the world,
Of the Blessed Mary, Ever Virgin,
By the Operation of the HOLY GHOST;
Spare us.

---

[1] *From the Collects, Secretæ, and Post Communion Prayers of the Gallican Missal.*

Whose Blessed Son, the Saviour of the World,
Being born, hath been to us
The Author of Heavenly birth;
Spare us.

Whose Only Son, Jesus Christ,
Offered Himself without Spot to Thee;
Spare us.

Look upon Thy people
Who celebrate these Mysteries,
In remembrance of that Immaculate Lamb,
Who poured forth the first drops of His Blood
For our sakes; &
Spare us.

The Light of faithful Souls,
Who hast hallowed the first dawn
Of the Election of the Gentiles;
Spare us.

Who, by Thy Only Begotten Son,
Who humbled Himself,
& became obedient unto death,
Hast subdued the pride of the ancient enemy;
Spare us.

Who

Who madeſt our LORD JESUS CHRIST
To ſit on the foal of an aſs,
& the people to ſpread their garments,
To ſtrew branches in the way,
& to cry, Hoſannah ;
Spare us.

May He cauſe our Oblation
To be acceptable to Thee,
Who delivered This Holy Rite
To His Diſciples,
For a Remembrance of Himſelf ;
Spare us.

Who, for our Redemption,
Didſt give Thy SON
To ſuffer Death upon the Croſs ;
Spare us.

Who, by His Glorious Reſurrection,
Haſt delivered us
From the power of the enemy ;
Spare us.

Give heed to our prayers
Who confeſs that JESUS CHRIST
Sitteth

OF THE ETERNAL FATHER.

Sitteth on the Right Hand of Thy Majesty; &
Spare us.

Cleanse our hearts, we pray Thee,
By the Indwelling of Thy HOLY SPIRIT; &
Spare us.

We sinners, do beseech Thee,
To hear us, O Heavenly FATHER;

That we may perceive
That He is with us alway,
According to His Promise,
Even unto the end of the world;
Grant us, Good LORD.

That we may so die daily unto sin,
That we may evermore live with Him,
In the Joy of His Resurrection;
Grant us.

That we may be conquerors over death,
In Him, and through Him,
Whose Members we are;
Grant us.

That we may meditate
Upon what He hath suffered for us;
& after

& after His example,
May patiently endure adversities;
Grant us.

That Thou manifest Thyself,
By the brightness of Thy Light;
Grant us.

That Thou purge our consciences
From dead works,
& make us, with Him, a Sacrifice
Acceptable to Thee;
Grant us.

That He may be to us,
The Fountain of everlasting Life
In the world to come;
Grant us.

That we may have Grace, to receive
The fruit of His Redemption,
Whose Incarnation is revealed;
Grant us.

That we may know,
That there is none other Name
Upon Whom we ought to call,

But

But only the Name of the LORD JESUS;
Grant us.

That Thou deliver us
From the bondage of sin,
& translate us to the glorious Liberty
Of the Sons of GOD;
Grant us.

That, by the inward Sprinkling of
The Grace of the HOLY SPIRIT
We may be fruitful in good works;
Grant us.

II.

O LORD, our Heavenly FATHER,
For the Coming of Whose SON,
With the ardent longing of our hearts,
We wait;
Spare us, Good LORD.

Whose Co-eternal, and Co-equal SON,
By the Ineffable Mystery of the Incarnation,
Took upon Him our Nature;
Spare us.

Grant

Grant us to receive
The New Light of the world, made Flesh; &
Spare us.

Who didst fulfil the expectation of
The devout Simeon,
In manifesting to him the LORD's CHRIST;
Spare us.

Behold the Oblations of Thy Church,
Amongst which,
Neither Gold, nor Frankincense, nor Myrrh,
Are offered,
But That Which is figured by them;
Spare us.

Whose Blessed SON,
By a solemn Fasting,
Entered upon the work of His Ministry;
Spare us.

Whose Only SON, in a desert place,
Did wonderfully feed
The multitude that came to Him;
Spare us.

Whose Only Begotten SON,

Having

Having loved His own, in the world,
Loved them unto the end;
Spare us.

The Death, & Paſſion of Whoſe Son,
We commemorate
In this Unbloody Sacrifice;
Spare us.

To Whom, by the Reſurrection of Jesus Christ,
We offer this our Solemn Sacrifice
Of Praiſe & Thankſgiving;
Spare us.

Who haſt brought again from the dead
That Great Shepherd of the ſheep,
Through the Blood of the Everlaſting Covenant;
Spare us.

Whoſe Bleſſed Son,
Our Merciful, & Faithful High Prieſt,
Having Aſcended into Heaven,
Ever liveth to make Interceſſion for us;
Spare us.

Whoſe Only Begotten Son, Christ,
At His Second Coming,

Shall appear in Glorious Majesty;
Spare us.

We sinners, do beseech Thee,
To hear us, O Heavenly FATHER,

That we may obtain Thy Succour,
In the present life;
& the Prize of Eternal Blessedness,
In the Life to come;
Grant us, good LORD.

That, by this Holy Sacrament,
Thou mayest make us partakers of
His Divine Nature;
Grant us.

That in our life, & conversation,
We may show the effect of that Faith,
Which shineth in our hearts;
Grant us.

That we, falling asleep in the LORD,
May, through Him, obtain Eternal Life;
Grant us.

That worshipping Him in the Holy Sacrament,
Whom

Whom the Wise Men worshipped
In the Manger,
We may, out of our hearts,
Bring Offerings acceptable to Thee;
Grant us.

That we, who in our Warfare,
Contend against spiritual wickedness,
May be strengthened by holy Abstinence;
Grant us.

That Thou bestow upon us,
In our passage through the world,
The Spiritual Sustenance
Of the FLESH & BLOOD of Thy Blessed SON;
Grant us.

That we may so meditate,
Upon the Mystery of His Love,
& so follow the example of His Humility;
That we may be united to Him
Who died for our sins;
& also follow Him,
Who rose again for our Justification;
Grant us.

That

That we may have in us,
The same Mind which was in Him;
Grant us.

That Thou grant to us,
Who feed on Him, our Passover,
The Unleavened **Bread**
Of Sincerity, & Truth;
Grant us.

That we, who approach in Faith
To the Throne of Grace,
May obtain Mercy, & find Grace,
To help, in time of need;
Grant us.

That Thou mercifully hear
The prayers of Thy people,
That they may obtain the prize
of Everlasting Life;
Grant us.

That Thou make us perfect
To do Thy Will, in every good work,
Working that which is pleasing in Thy Sight;
Grant us.

LITANIES OF OUR BLESSED LORD.

[*In Thankſgiving for the Moſt Holy Sacrament.*][1]

I.

O LORD JESU CHRIST,
High Prieſt, & Victim,
Who, of Thy unſpeakable Mercy,
Haſt vouchſafed to call us
Out of darkneſs, unto Thy marvellous Light;
JESU, Maſter, have mercy upon us.

Who haſt fed us with the Bleſſed Sacrament
Of Thy Moſt Precious BODY & BLOOD;
JESU, Maſter.

Who, in the Holy Communion,

---

[1] *From the Collects and Poſt Communion Prayers of the Paris Miſſal.*

Haſt

Haft wonderfully prepared ftrength,
For us who are haftening
To the Eternity which Thou haft promifed ;
JESU, Mafter.

Who haft given us to know,
& by Thy Holy Sacrament, to foretafte,
The Myfteries of Thy Kingdom ;
JESU, Mafter.

Who Alone doft know
The number of Thine Elect ;
JESU, Mafter.

Of Whom the whole Family
In Heaven, and earth is named ;
JESU, Mafter.

Who heareft the prayers of Thy Servants,
& doft quicken in them
The Germ of Righteoufnefs ;
JESU, Mafter.

Who Alone art Great amongft the great ;
& yet, amongft the leaft,
Doft glorioufly work marvels ;
JESU, Mafter.

Whose abundant Blessing descends,
Upon Thy people that prayeth unto Thee;
JESU, Master.

Who art the Light of all true hearts,
The perfect Light of the Saints,
& the Light of the Church;
JESU, Master.

Who, for the strengthening of our Souls,
Hast taught us to chasten our bodies
By holy Abstinence;
JESU, Master.

Who knowest the secrets of our hearts,
& searchest out all our ways;
JESU, Master.

Who seest that our affections
Are hindered by things of earth;
JESU, Master.

Who, for Thy Great Love's sake,
Didst offer Thyself for our Redemption,
As a Lamb without spot;
JESU, Master.

We

We sinners,
Beseech Thee,

That with meek hearts, we may discern,
& with due reverence receive,
Thy Holy Mysteries;
Remember us, LORD,
When Thou comest into Thy Kingdom.

That Thy Life-giving BODY
May heal the leprosy of our souls;
& that Thy BLOOD
May cleanse us from the pollution of sin;
Remember.

That, preserved from the darkness of error,
We may constantly walk
In the Light of Thy Truth;
Remember.

That Thou protect the frailty of Thy people
Amidst the tempests of the world;
& finally, bring us
Unto the Haven of Everlasting Salvation;
Remember.

That Thou so quicken, and sustain us,
That,

That, in the Great Day,
We may be ſeparated from the wicked,
& be numbered among Thine Elect;
Remember.

That we ſo run in the race of this life,
That we may obtain the prize
Of Thy Heavenly calling;
Remember.

That the names of all who have fed
Upon this Heavenly Food,
With thoſe for whom we pray,
May be written in the Book of Life;
Remember.

That we may love Thee Alone,
By Whoſe Blood we were redeemed,
& by Whoſe Grace we are juſtified;
Remember.

That the hope of Heavenly Joys
May ſuſtain us, who walk,
As ſtrangers and pilgrims,
Through the valley of the ſhadow of death;
Remember.

That

That we, who by Redemption,
Have attained the liberty of sons,
May be partakers of the eternal Inheritance;
Remember.

That the Gifts from Thy Altar
May kindle in our hearts,
The desire for the Heavenly Country;
Remember.

That Thou suffer not that to turn
To our condemnation,
Which Thou hast provided
For the health of the Faithful;
Remember.

That we, who in memory of Thy Passion,
Partake of This BREAD,
May, at the last day,
By Thee be raised, and live with Thee for ever;
Remember.

II.

O LORD JESU CHRIST,
High Priest, and Victim,

The

The Creator of the Univerſe,
According to Whoſe Will
The whole courſe of the world continueth;
JESU, Maſter, have mercy upon us.

Who haſt taught us,
That we cannot be partakers of Thy Table,
& of the table of devils;
JESU, Maſter.

Who haſt mercifully willed,
That there ſhould be joy in Heaven,
Over one ſinner that repenteth;
JESU, Maſter.

Who haſt given unto us the pledge
Of the Heavenly Inheritance;
JESU, Maſter.

Who doſt diſpel the darkneſs of ignorance
By the Light of Thy Word,
JESU, Maſter.

Who dwelleſt in the Heavens,
& Who will not forſake them
That are true of heart;
JESU, Maſter.

Who doſt never ceaſe,
Whilſt granting their prayers,
To cheriſh Thy people with Bleſſings;
JESU, Maſter.

Who, by preſent ſorrows,
Doſt correct us,
That Thou mayeſt bring us to future Joys;
& Who doſt comfort us
With temporal Bleſſings,
To aſſure us of Eternal Rewards;
JESU, Maſter.

Who doſt guide the ark of Thy Church
So that It is tried by adverſity,
& comforted by proſperity;
JESU, Maſter.

Who, perfecting ſtrength in weakneſs,
Haſt granted to Thy Church
To prevail, & be exalted,
When She ſeemed to be oppreſſed;
JESU, Maſter.

Who, by this Life-giving Food,
Doſt vouchſafe unto us,

While

While sojourners on earth,
To be partakers of Heavenly Things;
JESU, Master.

Who art Merciful in Thy Works,
Just in Thy Judgments,
& Bountiful in Thy Gifts;
We sinners,
Beseech Thee.

That Thou cherish in us
What Thou dost give us;
& that Thou mayest find in us
What Thou wilt reward;
Remember us, LORD,
When Thou comest into Thy Kingdom.

That we who have been nourished,
With these Saving Mysteries,
May, through the Power of the Same,
Offer ourselves a living Sacrifice;
Remember.

That we, who have now been fed
With Spiritual Food, Which is CHRIST,
May, by the Power of Thy Might,

The

The Sword of the SPIRIT, & Shield of Faith,
Overcome the snares of the enemy;
Remember.

That we may obtain Thy Succour
Both in body and Soul;
& that, being strengthened in both,
We may rejoice in the fulness of
Thy Heavenly Blessing;
Remember.

That Thou so rule & govern us
In the life we now live,
That Thou mayest bring us to the Light
In which Thou dwellest for ever;
Remember.

That affliction may prove, in us,
The firmness of our Faith;
& by Thy Help, our Devotion
May triumph against all adversities;
Remember.

That the Power of Thy Heavenly Gift
May fill our Souls and bodies;
& that not our reason, but Thy Grace,
May

May always prevail in us;
Remember.

That Thou mercifully grant unto us
Who are partakers of this Sacrifice,
That the ears of our heart be opened
To the obedience of Thy Word,
& our tongues be loosed
To glorify Thy Name;
Remember.

That this Holy Sacrament
Impart to us, that humility of heart,
Whereby Thou doft renew
Sinners unto Righteousness;
& doft advance
The Righteous unto Glory;
Remember.

That we, confessing Thee,
Not in word, or in tongue only,
But also, in deed, & in Truth,
May be made meet for the Kingdom of Heaven;
Remember.

That we, whom Thou haft fed
With Heavenly Mysteries,

May

May be cleansed from our secret sins,
& delivered from the snares of our enemies;
Remember.

That we, who put not our trust
In anything that we do,
May, with humble confession,
Ascribe the fruit of our labour
To the Glory of Thy Name;
Remember.

That, by the Power of this Sacrament,
We may be united to Thee
The Good Shepherd;
& also, may thankfully rejoice
For the return of the sheep that were lost;
Remember.

That we may be ever numbered
Amongst Thy Members,
In Whose BODY we communicate;
Remember.

LITANIES OF OUR BLESSED LORD.

[*Eucharistic Prayers for the Sundays in Lent.*]¹

I.

We ask forgiveness; CHRIST, hear us;
Be appeased, & have pity.

JESU, Only Begotten SON of GOD the FATHER, Who art the LORD of boundless Goodness;
Be appeased.

We all beseech Thee, craving it with groans; we all jointly entreating, pray;
Be appeased.

Now let Thy Clemency repair our evils; now look on us with Thy gracious Face;
Be appeased.

---
¹ *From the Mozarabic Liturgy of S. Isidore.*

Graciously

Gracioufly remove from us Thy wrath; put an end to fin; give reft from evil;
Be appeafed.

Tranquillity of times; abundance of good things; quiet peace; plenteous health;
Be appeafed.

Beftow Thy aid on the Bifhop ——, and on Thy fuppliant people;
Be appeafed.

We afk remiffion of all fins; mercifully forgive the evils we have committed;
Be appeafed.

II.

Have mercy, & fpare Thy people, moft Clement LORD;
Becaufe we have finned againft Thee.

Proftrate, we all pour forth tears; laying open to Thee our fecret faults; of Thee, O GOD, we afk pardon;
Becaufe.

Receive the prayers of Thy Priefts; & richly beftow

bestow all that they ask; & pity Thy people, O LORD;
Because.

Thou hast brought Thy anger over us; our dire offences have bowed us down; & we have fainted, without any hope;
Because.

We have been given up to evils which we knew not; & every evil is rushing in upon us; & we call on Thee, & we have not hearkened unto Thee;
Because.

We all cry aloud; we all intreat; we seek Thee with tears of penitence, Whose wrath we have ourselves provoked;
Because.

Intreating Thee, we beg of Thee, with lamentation; Thee, JESUS CHRIST, we prostrate seek; let Thy Power now relieve the miserable;
Because.

Receive the confession of Thy people, which
we

we lamenting, pour out before Thee; & we groan in heart for our offences;
Because.

Peace we ask; peace vouchsafe us; remove wars, & rescue us all; with humble prayer we implore Thee, LORD;
Because.

Incline Thine ear, O most Clement GOD; now shall the stains of our sins be washed away; & do Thou benignantly deliver us from danger;
Have pity, & spare.

III.

We pray Thee, Holy GOD, Eternal King;
Now have mercy; we have sinned against Thee.

Hear our cry, most High FATHER; & mercifully grant our requests; hear us, O LORD;
Now.

O Good REDEEMER, we humbly pray; weeping from our whole heart, we pray Thee graciously be present with us;
Now.

Send

Send out Thy Hand, O GOD Almighty; & powerfully protect from on high those who call upon Thee, O most Loving;
Now.

Grant us fruitful lands, & peace; remove wars; restrain famines, O REDEEMER Most Holy;
Now.

Forgive the fallen; forgive the lost; put away hurtful things; wash out crimes; do Thou deliver those who are bowed down;
Now.

Look on us groaning; consider our weeping; extend Thy Hand; redeem the sinners;
Now.

Receive, O GOD, this our prayer; favourably receive the voices of the suppliants; & spare, O most Loving;
We pray Thee now have mercy.

IV.

IV.

Behold, O Lord, my humiliation, because the enemy hath been lifted up;

Have mercy, O Righteous FATHER; & grant forgiveness to all.

"Sent from the FATHER, I came to seek the lost; & to redeem with Blood those captured by the enemy: the terrible people cast Me away;"

Have mercy.

"Foretold by Prophets, I was born of the Virgin; I assumed the form of a Servant, to gather the dispersed; the hunters took Me;"

Have mercy.

"Unto Me for good, many evils were returned; against Me sold for money, they gave unrighteous counsels;"

Have mercy.

"They set a Crown of Thorns on My Head, which was defiled with spitting; the impious scoffed at Me when cruelly afflicted;"

Have mercy.

"With

OF OUR BLESSED LORD.

" With guilty robbers, hung on a Gibbet; fed with bitter food, and bitter cup; given over to execution;"

Have mercy.

" They whom I came to deliver, accused Me; they lashed Me with scourges, and nailed Me to the Cross; with a spear they pierced Me;"

Have mercy.

O Thou, Who didst put away the guilt of an impious robber, do Thou loose our chains, remit our sins, save us by Thy Cross;

Have mercy.

" I was delivered to the Sepulchre; I burst the gates of hell; I cast out those that were bound, and brought them back on high; I showed Myself in Sacrifice;"

Have mercy.

" Most Clement FATHER, forgive them all offences; wash out sins; and remit the crimes of those who know not what they do;"

Have mercy.

V.

V.

"Mine adversaries laid snares for Me without a cause;"

Thou, Holy FATHER, have mercy, & deliver me.

"I was led as an innocent Lamb to the Sacrifice; I was taken by enemies, as a bird in a snare; sorely without cause;"

Thou, Holy FATHER.

"All of them opened their mouths against Me; they gnashed upon Me with their teeth; seeking to deliver me; sorely without cause;"

Thou, Holy FATHER.

"They cried aloud, hissing; & they shook their heads; taking in hand to bring forth false witnesses against Me; sorely without cause;"

Thou, Holy FATHER.

"They condemn Me; & hang Me on the Cross, fixed with iron nails; sold by the Jews for thirty pieces of silver; sorely without cause;"

Thou, Holy FATHER.

"I was

"I was pierced in the Side by a horrible spear; thence flows Water, with innocent Blood; sorely without cause;"

Thou, Holy FATHER.

"They all came upon Me, like a flood of waters, & I was plunged in the Sepulchre; they laid a stone upon it; sorely without cause;"

Thou, Holy FATHER.

"All the stars of Heaven grew pale with confusion; the day is wrapped in darkness when it sees its LORD suffer; sorely without cause;"

Thou, Holy FATHER.

"So the multitude of the Jews, with blind mistrust, ask of Pilate a band of soldiers; sorely without cause;"

Thou, Holy FATHER.

"Then the soldiers divide My Vesture by lot; gazing at the unrighteous & savage blows laid upon Me; sorely without cause;"

Thou, Holy FATHER.

"Give ear, O loving FATHER, & succour the miserable

miserable, for whom I am afflicted with such bitter punishments; sorely without cause;"
Thou, Holy FATHER.

VI.

Remember us, O CHRIST, in Thy Kingdom; & make us worthy of Thy Resurrection.

" With desire I have desired to eat this Passover with you;"
Before I suffer.

" Go ye, & prepare us the Passover, that we may eat;"
Before I suffer.

" Behold, when ye go into the City . . . . say ye to the good man of the house ——;"
Before I suffer.

" The Master saith, My time is at hand, where is . . . . with My Disciples;"
Before I suffer.

" & he will show you . . . . make ready the Passover;"
Before I suffer.

& the

& the Disciples went .... made ready the Passover;

With desire, I have desired.

& when even was come, Jesus .... said unto them;

With desire.

" For I say unto you .... in the Kingdom of God;"

With desire.

He took Bread, & blessed, & brake .... & said unto them;

With desire.

" Take, Eat, THIS IS .... This do ye;"

With desire.

Likewise also, the Cup .... saying, " Take This;" & He gave thanks .... saying —;

With desire.

" Drink ye all of This, for THIS IS .... for the remission of sins;"

With desire.

Glory & honour to FATHER, SON, HOLY SPIRIT, for ever & ever. Amen.

With desire.

LITANIES OF OUR LORD JESUS CHRIST.

[*On the Gifts & Graces of the Holy Communion.*]¹

I.

O CHRIST,
The King,
Eternal, Immortal, Invisible,
Who on His Vesture, & on His Thigh
Hath a Name written,
King of kings, and LORD of lords;
*Wash me throughly from my wickedness,
& cleanse me from my sin.*

The MASTER,
Who layeth on His servants
The sweet Yoke, & light Burden of

---
¹ *From the Eucharistic Month.*

His Commands, & Counsels;
Wash me.

The MASTER,
Who teacheth us what is profitable for us;
Wash me.

The Faithful FRIEND,
Whom nothing doth countervail;
& Who, instead of enemies,
Hath made us very dear friends;
Wash me.

A BROTHER,
Who, though He be Very GOD, & LORD
of all men,
Is not ashamed to call us brethren;
Wash me.

The Everlasting FATHER,
Who, of His Own Will, hath begotten us
With the Word of Truth;
Wash me.

The BRIDEGROOM,
Who hath said:
I will betroth thee unto Me,

In Righteousness, Judgment,
Loving-kindness, & Mercy;
Wash me.

The SUN of Righteousness,
The Brightness of Glory, & the True Light
That lighteth every man that cometh
Into the world;
Wash me.

The Pilgrim's PROVISION,
The Medicine of Immortality,
& the Earnest of Eternal Glory;
Wash me.

The FEASTER, & the FEAST;
A Feast of fat things,
A Feast of Wine on the lees,
Of fat things full of Marrow,
Of Wine on the lees well refined;
Wash me.

The BELOVED,
White, & Ruddy;
White, under the appearance of Bread;
Ruddy, under the appearance of Wine;
Chiefest

Chiefest among ten thousand;
& altogether Lovely;
Wash me.

The HEIR,
Who, though He was Rich,
Yet, for our sakes, He became Poor;
That we, through His Poverty, might be Rich;
Wash me.

The WINE,
Which the LORD hath prepared,
For those who are sad at heart,
That they may drink, & forget their poverty,
& remember their misery no more;
Wash me.

We sinners, beseech Thee,
To hear us, O LORD GOD;

That it may please Thee, to grant us
A clean Heart
That, the eyes of our mind being purified,
We may be raised to the contemplation of
Thy Beauty;
Grant this, Gracious LORD.

The Virtue of Justice,
That putting aside all avarice, we may
Render unto Cæsar, the things that are Cæsar's,
& unto God, the things that are God's;
Grant.

The Virtue of Temperance,
That we may reign over, & repress
All lustful desires,
& may moderate ourselves in all things;
Grant.

The Gift of Charity,
That God Alone may be sweet to us,
& that all other things may be tasteless;
Grant.

The Gift of Stedfast Hope,
That we may, with boldness, say:
I will lay me down in peace,
& take my rest,
For Thou Lord Only, makest me dwell in safety;
Grant.

The Gift of Faith,
That we may perceive what we ought to do,
& have

& have strength to fulfil the same;
Grant.

The SPIRIT of Wisdom,
That we may search out the hidden things of GOD,
To excite a greater love for Him in our hearts;
Grant.

The SPIRIT of Obedience,
That we may diligently inquire our duty,
& perform it in the sight of all;
Grant.

The SPIRIT of Understanding,
That we may ever understand
The hidden meanings of H. Scripture;
Grant.

The SPIRIT of Counsel,
That we may ever choose
Fit remedies for the Salvation of our Souls;
Grant.

The SPIRIT of Knowledge,
That we may ever discern
Between Truth, & falsehood,

& con-

& constantly hold fast the Profession of Faith;
Grant.

The SPIRIT of Fear of the LORD,
That we may flee every sin,
& fear Him Alone, with pure affection;
Grant.

The SPIRIT of Fortitude,
That we may defend the Divine Honour,
Even unto death;
Grant.

II.

O CHRIST,
The BREAD of GOD,
That came down from Heaven,
& giveth life unto the world;
*Wash me throughly from my wickedness,
& cleanse me from my sin.*

The HIGH PRIEST,
Holy, Harmless, Undefiled, separate from sinners,
& made higher than the Heavens;

Who

Who offered up prayers & supplications,
With strong crying & tears;
Wash me.

The MAN of Sorrows,
& acquainted with grief,
Who was wounded for our transgressions,
& bruised for our iniquities;
Wash me.

A Consuming FIRE,
Who maketh His Angels Spirits,
& His Ministers a flaming Fire;
Wash me.

The Skilful PHYSICIAN,
Who hath borne our griefs,
& carried our sorrows;
Wash me.

The PEARL of great Price,
For Which, if a man gave all his substance,
It would be utterly contemned;
Wash me.

The TREE of Life,
Bearing twelve manner of Fruits,
& yield-

& yielding His Fruit every month;
The leaves Whereof are for the healing of the nations;
Wash me.

The LEADER of the People, & LORD of Hosts,
Who came not to send peace, but a sword;
Wash me.

The WELL of Life,
A Fountain opened for sin & uncleanness,
That he that is athirst may come,
& that whoso will, may take of the Water freely;
Wash me.

The REDEEMER,
Who hast redeemed us from our conversation
With His Own precious BLOOD;
Wash me.

The SHEPHERD of Souls,
Who knoweth His Own sheep,
& layeth down His Life for them;
Wash me.

The EXEMPLAR
Of all Holiness & Virtue,
That was once shown forth on Calvary,

& is

& is now daily, in the H. Eucharist;
Wash me.

We sinners, beseech Thee,
To hear us, O LORD GOD.

That it may please Thee to grant us
Conformity to the Divine Will,
That Thou mayest be able to boast,
I have found a man after Mine Own Heart;
Grant this, Gracious LORD.

The Virtue of Religion,
That we may render unto Thee
The worship, honour, & reverence
That is due unto Thee;
Grant.

The Virtue of Brotherly Love,
That, as Thou didst lay down Thy Life for us,
So we also may lay down our lives for the
Brethren;
Grant.

The Virtue of Humility,
For Thou sendest springs into the valleys
That run among the hills;
Thou givest Grace unto the humble,
& re-

& resisteth the proud;
Grant.

The Virtue of Self-denial,
That we may not run uncertainly,
Nor fight as one that beateth the air;
But may keep under the body,
& bring it into subjection;
Grant.

The Virtue of Watchfulness,
That we never cease to purge the Soul from vices,
& to adorn it with Virtue;
Grant.

The Virtue of Prayer,
In such wise, that asking, we may receive,
Seeking, we may find,
Knocking, it may be opened unto us;
Grant.

The Virtue of Obedience,
That we may follow the example of Him
Who became obedient unto death;
Grant.

Perfect Peace,
That resting in Thee,

We

We may be esteemed true Peacemakers,
Who shall be called Sons of GOD;
Grant.

Hunger & Thirst after Righteousness,
That aiming at a more perfect State,
We may attain the everlasting fruition
Of Thy Presence;
Grant.

A Life-giving Sorrow,
That as Thy Sufferings abound in us,
So, our consolation may abound in Thee;
Grant.

Bowels of Mercy,
That we may obtain mercy from Him,
Who being tempted in all points as we are,
Can be touched with the feeling of our infirmities;
Grant.

Poverty of Spirit,
That, renouncing all things,
We may, without let or hindrance,
Run along the path of Perfection
That leadeth to the Kingdom of Heaven;
Grant.

LITANIES OF JESU CHRIST.

[*On the Holy Sacrament.*]¹

I.

JESU CHRIST,
WORD of the FATHER, SON of the Virgin,
Lamb of GOD, Salvation of the world,
H. Sacrifice,
WORD in Flesh, Fountain of Pity;
Spare us, Good LORD, Spare us,
We most humbly beseech Thee.

Praise of Angels, Glory of Saints,
Vision of Peace,
Entire DEITY, True Man,
Flower and Fruit of the Virgin Mother;
Spare us.

---

¹ *From the Enchiridion or Hours, & the Missal, of the English Use of Sarum.*

Brightness

Brightness of the FATHER,
Prince of Peace, Gate of Heaven,
Living BREAD,
Offspring of the Virgin, Vessel of the GOD-head;
Spare us.

Light of Heaven, Ransom of the world,
Joy of our hearts, Bread of Angels,
King & Spouse of Virginity;
Spare us.

The Most Sweet Way, Supreme Truth,
Reward of ours,
Living Charity, Fountain of Love, Peace,
& Sweetness of Eternal Life;
Spare us.

Most Holy, & Precious BODY,
Set on the Altar of the Cross
For the Saving of the world,
True Sacrifice, Pure Sacrifice, H. Sacrifice,
Unspotted & acceptable unto GOD;
Spare us.

The Holy BREAD of Eternal Life,
& the CUP of Everlasting Salvation;
Spare us.

By

By the Virtue of Thy Holy Cross;
Good LORD, deliver us.

By the Mystery of Thy Holy Incarnation;
Good LORD.

By Thy Nativity, Baptism, & Fasting;
Good LORD.

By Thy Passion, Death, Resurrection, Ascension;
Good LORD.

By the Coming of the HOLY GHOST;
Good LORD.

By Thy Name Ineffable,
Thou Who art GOD Almighty;
Good LORD.

Alpha & Omega, the Beginning & the End;
Good LORD.

Sabaoth, Adonai, Emmanuel,
Which is GOD with us;
Good LORD.

The Way, the Truth, the Life,
Our Salvation, Victory, & Resurrection;
Good LORD.

By

By the Life-giving Sacrifice
Of Thy BODY & BLOOD;
Good LORD.

We sinners,
Beseech Thee;

That we so venerate these S. Mysteries,
That we may perceive in ourselves,
The Fruit of Thy Redemption;
We beseech Thee hear us.

That Thou incline Thy Ears to our prayers,
& enlighten our hearts
With the Grace of Thy HOLY SPIRIT;
We beseech Thee.

That we may worthily celebrate
Thy Holy Mysteries,
& love Thee with an everlasting Love;
We beseech Thee.

That we may offer Sacrifices,
Pleasing & acceptable unto Thee,
For all our sins & offences;
We beseech Thee.

That we may approach This H. Sacrament,
With that pureness of heart & cleanness of mind,
With that devotion & reverence,
Which becometh us;
We beseech Thee.

That it be the purgation of our spiritual sloth,
The cleansing of our offences,
& our protection against all perils;
We beseech Thee.

That Thy B. Body & Blood
May be the remission of our sins,
The putting away of evil thoughts,
The renewal of good desires,
The healthful effectuating
Of works well pleasing unto Thee,
& the firm protection of Soul & body
Against the wiles of our enemies;
We beseech Thee.

That Thou vouchsafe to heal our infirmities,
To wash away our defilements,
To enlighten our blindness,
To enrich our poverty,

& to

& to clothe our nakedness;
We beseech Thee.

That Thou wouldest restore the wandering,
Console the forsaken, reconcile the guilty,
Grant pardon to the sinner,
Forgiveness to the wretched, life to the criminal,
& righteousness to the dead;
We beseech Thee.

That we may receive Thee with
That chastity of body & purity of soul,
That contrition of heart & fountain of tears,
Spiritual gladness & celestial joy,
With that fear & awe, reverence & honour,
That faith & humility, purpose & love,
& with that devotion, & thankfulness,
Which is expedient for the health of our souls;
We beseech Thee.

That we may receive not only the Sacrament
Of Thy Most Precious BODY & BLOOD,
But also the Substance & Virtue of that Sacrament;
We beseech Thee.

That we may be found worthy

To

To be incorporated into Thy Myſtical BODY,
& reckoned among Thy Members;
We beſeech Thee.

That Whom we now receive beneath a Veil,
In this our pilgrimage,
We may at length, with unveiled face,
Contemplate for ever;
We beſeech Thee.

II.

JESU CHRIST,
Delectable Bread, Repaſt of Life,
Food much to be deſired,
Banquet of exceeding Sweetneſs,
Refreſhing all things, & never-failing;
Spare us, Good LORD, Spare us,
We moſt humbly beſeech Thee.

King of Virgins, Lover of Chaſtity,
Supreme Phyſician, Terrible Majeſty,
Fountain of Mercy,
Life-giving Victim;
Spare us.

True

True Charity, Immaculate Sacrifice,
Food of the hungry, Bread of Angels,
King of kings, & LORD of lords;
Spare us.

Fount of pity,
Prince of Angels, Glory of the Saints,
Hope of sinners;
Spare us.

Light of the world, Word of the FATHER,
Very Sacrifice, Flesh of Life,
Entire Deity, Very Man;
Spare us.

Principle of creation, Price of Redemption,
Viaticum of our pilgrimage,
Comfort of expectation, Surety of Salvation;
Spare us.

By Thy excelling Love
Wherewith Thou didst love mankind,
When hanging on the Altar of the Cross;
Good LORD, deliver us.

By Thy Divine Charity, & compassionate Soul;
By Thy most sad condition;

By

By Thy troubled Senses, & pierced Heart;
Good LORD.

By Thy stricken Members, & scourged Body;
Thy gory Wounds, & streams of Blood;
Thy outstretched Arms, & transfixed Feet;
Good LORD.

By Thy swollen Veins;
By Thy wailing Mouth, & hoarse Voice;
Thy pallid Face, & deadly paleness;
By Thy tearful Eyes, & swimming Brain;
Good LORD.

By Thy burning Love;
By Thy moaning Throat, & parched Thirst;
By Thy bitter Taste of vinegar & gall;
Good LORD.

By Thy approaching Death;
By the dividing of Thy BODY & SOUL;
By Thy rent Side,
The source of the living Fountain;
Good LORD.

By Thy Love,
O most pitiful & sweetest LORD JESU,

We

We sinners,
Beseech Thee.

That our Soul may taste
How sweet the LORD is;
& that at the taste of Thee
All carnal delights may give place;
We beseech Thee, hear us.

That, in our pilgrimage,
Our sinful Souls faithfully partake of Thee;
& so receive strength from Thee,
That we perform our journey unto Thee,
Without hindrance from Satan;
We beseech Thee.

That Thou take from us
All our iniquities & sins,
That we may be made worthy, worthily
To taste the HOLY of Holies;
We beseech Thee.

That, trusting in Thy Goodness,
We may approach Thy Altar,
To the Sacrament of Thy BODY & BLOOD;
We beseech Thee.

That we may come,
Sick, to the Physician of Life;
Unclean, to the Fountain of Mercy;
Blind, to the Light of eternal Splendour;
We beseech Thee.

That we may draw near,
Poor, to the LORD of Heaven & earth;
Naked, to the King of Glory;
Sheep, to the Shepherd; creatures, to the Creator;
We beseech Thee.

That we may approach
Desolate, to the kind Comforter;
Miserable, to the Pitier;
Guilty, to the Bestower of Pardon;
Wicked, to the Justifier;
Hardened, to the Infuser of Grace;
We beseech Thee.

That Thou wouldest mortify
In our members & in our hearts,
All incitements of the flesh,
& all hurtful passions;
We beseech Thee.

That Thy BODY broken,
May be unto us, the remiſſion of
All our ſins, negligences, and ignorances;
We beſeech Thee.

That Thy BLOOD poured out,
May be unto us, Strength,
For the increaſe of Faith, Hope, & Charity,
& all other Graces, & Virtues;
We beſeech Thee.

That Thou wouldeſt forgive
The multitude of our offences;
& of Thy bountiful Mercy's ſake,
Wouldeſt vouchſafe to grant us
A good & holy ending to our life,
& a glorious, & joyful Reſurrection;
We beſeech Thee.

That What Thou haſt given
To blot out the ſins of mankind,
May not be in us
An increaſe of our offences,
But may be for our pardon & protection;
We beſeech Thee.

That

That we may so receive Thy Body & Blood,
That, by Thy Strength,
We may be fashioned into the likeness of
Thy Death & Resurrection;
We beseech Thee.

That, by mortification of the old man,
& renewal to a holy life,
We may be incorporated into
Thy Body, the Church;
& that we may become Thy Members,
& Thou, our Head;
We beseech Thee.

A LITANY OF THE LORD JESU CHRIST.

[*On the Holy Eucharist.*][1]

O LORD JESU CHRIST,
SON of the Living GOD,
Who, for our Redemption,
Didst will to be born;
*LORD, remember me
When Thou comest into Thy Kingdom.*

Who didst will to be circumcised;
To be rejected by the Jews;
To be betrayed by Judas, with a kiss;
& to be taken bound in chains;
LORD, remember.

---

[1] *From the Devotions of S. Ambrose, & other ancient sources.*

Who didſt will to be haled before
Annas, Caiaphas, Herod, & Pilate;
LORD, remember.

& in their preſence to be mocked,
& to be ſmitten with
Blows, buffets, ſtripes, & the reed;
LORD, remember.

To be ſpitted on in the Face;
To be crowned with thorns;
To be accuſed of falſe witneſſes;
To be judged;
& as a Lamb, to be led as a Victim;
LORD, remember.

Who didſt will to be pierced with nails;
To be made to drink of vinegar & gall;
& upon the Croſs,
To be condemned to a moſt ſhameful Death;
LORD, remember.

From all evils, at all times;
Good LORD, deliver us.

From injury, & ſnares;
From

From captivity, & bonds;
& from the tongues, & weapons, & shafts
Of all our enemies,
Visible & invisible;
Good LORD.

From all wicked works;
From poisonous, & deadly food;
From shame, disease, confusion, slander;
& from all offences, & dangers;
Good LORD.

From all falling, ruin, hurt,
Detriment, & hindrance,
Of Soul & of body;
& from sudden, unforeseen, & eternal death;
Good LORD.

From all tribulation, & distress;
From all grief, & sadness;
From all danger, & wretchedness;
& from all sin, & impurity of heart;
Good LORD.

From all defiling, & unholy,

From

From all vain, & hurtful thoughts;
Good LORD.

From the hard spirit of pride, & vain glory;
From envy, & blasphemy;
From impurity, & uncleanness;
& from doubting, & mistrust;
Good LORD.

We sinners, do beseech Thee;
To hear us, O LORD GOD.

That we, through Thy Grace,
May always so believe, & understand,
So conceive, & firmly hold,
So think, & so speak,
Of that exceeding Mystery,
As shall please Thee, & be good for our Souls;
We pray Thee to hear us.

That Thy Good SPIRIT may enter our hearts,
& be heard without utterance;
& may speak all Truth,
Without the sound of words;
We pray Thee.

That,

OF THE LORD JESU CHRIST.

That, with contrition of heart,
& fountain of tears;
With reverence, & awe;
& with purity of mind, & body,
We may celebrate Thy H. Mysteries;
We pray Thee.

That we may approach this H. Sacrifice
With fear, & trembling;
With cleanness of heart, & streams of tears;
With spiritual gladness, & Heavenly joy;
We pray Thee.

That, through our unworthiness,
The price of their Salvation be not wasted,
For whom Thou hast vouchsafed to be
A saving Victim, & Redemption;
We pray Thee.

That Thou graciously behold
The tribulation of the People,
The groans of Prisoners,
& the miseries of Orphans;
We pray Thee.

That Thou mercifully relieve

The necessities of Strangers,
The helplessness of the Weak,
The depressions of the Languishing,
& the infirmities of the Aged;
We pray Thee.

That Thou favourably listen to
The aspirations of Young Men,
The vows of Virgins,
& the sorrows of the Widow;
We pray Thee.

That Thou take from us
The heart of stone;
& that Thou give unto us
A heart of flesh,
To love Thee, choose Thee, delight in Thee,
To follow Thee, & to enjoy Thee;
We pray Thee.

That this great Sacrament
Of Thy Love
May be, to the Souls of the Faithful Departed,
Health & Salvation,
Joy & Refreshment;
We pray Thee.

That

That Thou cleanse the palate of our Heart;
That we taste the sweetness of Thy Love;
That Thou ever refresh, & never fail us;
That we feed on Thee, & be filled with Thee;
& that Thou satisfy us with Thyself,
Who, with the FATHER and the SPIRIT,
Livest, & reignest,
For ever & ever;
We pray Thee.

A LITANY OF OUR BLESSED LORD JESUS CHRIST, PRIEST, AND VICTIM FOR MEN.

[*Based on the Doctrine of S. Paul's Epistle to the Hebrews.*]

JESUS, High Priest;
Have mercy upon us.
SON of GOD;
Have.

Taken from among men;
Have.

Over the House of GOD;
Have.

Ordained for men, in things pertaining to GOD;
Have.

Author, & Finisher of our Faith;
Have.

Of our Profession;
Have.

Who didst not glorify Thyself;
Have.

Made by Him that said: Thou art My Son, &c.;
Have.

Made, not after the law of a carnal command, but after the power of an endless Life;
Have.

Whom, not the law, but the Gospel hath perfected for ever;
Have.

Whom God hath anointed with the Holy Ghost, & with Power;
Have.

Called of God, after the Order of Melchisedec;
Have.

Who, when Thou camest into the world, didst say: Burnt Offerings & Sacrifice, &c.;
Have.

Tempted,

Tempted, in all points, like as we are, yet without sin;
Have.

Who canst have compassion on our infirmities;
Have.

Who, because Thou abidest ever, hast an everlasting Priesthood;
Have.

Who needest not daily to offer Sacrifice, but hast done this once, in offering Thyself;
Have.

Minister of the Sanctuary, & of the true Tabernacle;
Have.

Who hast obtained a more excellent Ministry than that of Aaron;
Have.

Who, through the Eternal SPIRIT, hast offered Thyself, without spot to GOD;
Have.

Who hast offered Thyself, to purge our consciences

sciences from dead works, to serve the Living GOD;
Have.

Mediator of the New Testament, Who, by Thy Death, hast made an Atonement;
Have.

Who didst offer Prayers & Supplications, with strong crying & tears;
Have.

Who wast heard, in that Thou didst fear;
Have.

Who hast entered into Heaven, that we may hold fast our Profession;
Have.

Of Good Things to come, of a greater & more perfect Tabernacle, not made with hands;
Have.

Who, not by the blood of bulls & goats, but by Thine Own BLOOD hast entered once into the Holy Place;
Have.

Who

· Who haft entered into Heaven itfelf, & not into Holy Places made with hands;
Have.

Who haft fat down on the Throne of the Majefty on High;
Have.

Holy, Harmlefs, Undefiled, & feparate from finners, & made higher than the Heavens;
Have.

Who, a fecond time, wilt appear to them that look for Thee, without fin, unto Salvation;
Have.

Who art able to fave to the uttermoft;
Have.

Who ever liveft to make interceffion;
Have.

Who, being made perfect, haft become a caufe of falvation to all that obey Thee;
Have.

By the offering of Whofe Body, & the fhedding of Whofe Blood without the gate, we are fanctified;
Have.

Who,

Who, by one Offering, haſt perfected them that are ſanctified;
Have.

By Whoſe BLOOD, we have boldneſs to enter into the Holieſt; & by Whoſe BODY, Thou haſt opened a new and living Way;
Have.

By Whoſe BLOOD, Heavenly things are purified, & the New Teſtament is dedicated and confirmed;
Have.

Through Whom, we offer continually the Sacrifice of Thankſgiving;
Have.

Who didſt take Bread, & break, & ſay: Take, &c.; & alſo the Cup, ſaying: This Cup, &c.;
Have.

Who didſt command: This do in remembrance of Me;
Have.

Who haſt made us Kings, & Prieſts to GOD, & the FATHER;
Have.

Who, by Thy Priesthood, hast glorified Thy FATHER upon earth;
Have.

Who hast finished the Work that was given Thee to do;
Have.

Who lovest the Church, & didst give Thyself for It; & hast sanctified, & cleansed It;
Have.

Through Whom we can come boldly to the Throne of Grace; & receive Mercy, & find Grace to help in every time of need;
Have.

Yesterday, now, & for ever, Priest, & Victim; & Whom, as Victim & Priest, we cannot understand, but can love;
Have.

A LIT-

A LITANY OF THE LORD JESU, PRIEST AND VICTIM.

[*Based on the Doctrine of S. Paul's Epistle to the Hebrews.*]

Jesu, High Priest for ever;
 Spare us, Good LORD.

Jesu, Great High Priest;
 Spare.

Jesu, High Priest for men;
 Spare.

Jesu, Faithful High Priest;
 Spare.

Jesu, Merciful High Priest;
 Spare.

Jesu, Beneficial High Priest;
 Spare.

Jesu, Perfect High Priest;
 Spare.

Jesu, High Priest, kindled with zeal for God, & Souls ;
Spare.

Jesu, Who fittest at the Right Hand of God ;
Spare.

Jesu, Who appearest in the Presence of God ;
Spare.

Jesu, Who hast opened a new, & living Way ;
Spare.

Jesu, Who hast loved us, & washed us in Thy Blood ;
Spare.

Jesu, Who hast made us Kings, & Priests ;
Spare.

Jesu, Sacrifice of God, & Man ;
Spare.

Jesu, Victim without spot ;
Spare.

Jesu, accepted Victim ;
Spare.

Jesu, Victim that appeasest the Father ;
Spare.

JESU, accustomed Sacrifice;
   Spare.

JESU, Mighty Victim;
   Spare.

JESU, Sacrifice of thanksgiving;
   Spare.

JESU, Peace Offering;
   Spare.

JESU, Sacrifice of Propitiation;
   Spare.

JESU, Sacrifice of Reconciliation;
   Spare.

JESU, Victim of Salvation;
   Spare.

JESU, Victim slain from the foundation of the world;
   Spare.

JESU, Victim, Who livest for ever & ever;
   Spare.

Be merciful;
   Spare us, Good LORD.

Be merciful;
Deliver us, Good LORD.

By Thy endless Priesthood;
Deliver us, Good LORD.

By Thy holy Anointing;
Deliver.

By the SPIRIT of the Priesthood;
Deliver.

By Thy Ministry;
Deliver.

By that Bloody Offering of Thyself, once made upon the Cross;
Deliver.

By that Sacrifice continually represented to the FATHER, in the Most Holy Eucharist;
Deliver.

By that Divine Power, which Thou the Only, & Unseen Priest dost exercise, in the Priests of Thy Church;
Deliver.

That

That Thou keep all Orders of Clergy in the True Religion;
Hear us, Good LORD.

That the SPIRIT of Thy Priesthood may be found in them;
Hear.

That the lips of Thy Priests may keep knowledge;
Hear.

That Thou send into Thy Harvest, Labourers who cannot be put to confusion;
Hear.

That Thou make Thy Ministers a Flame of Fire;
Hear.

That Thou raise up Pastors after Thine Own Heart;
Hear.

That Thy Priests be without spot, & blameless;
Hear.

That they who behold the Miniſters of Thy Altar, may glorify GOD;
Hear.

That they may offer to Thee Sacrifice, in Righteouſneſs;
Hear.

That by them, Thou promote reverence for Thy Moſt Bleſſed BODY & BLOOD;
Hear.

A LITANY OF THE LORD JESUS.

[*Before Holy Communion.*][1]

I have sought Thee with my whole heart;
LORD JESUS.

Help me, set me free from the bands of my sins;
LORD JESUS.

Help me, for Thou art able to save me;
LORD JESUS.

And Thou art Good, & ready to uphold;
LORD JESUS.

Take me under the shadow of Thy Wings;
LORD JESUS.

In six days Thou didst create all things;
LORD JESUS.

---

[1] *From a Copto-Arabic MS.*

Seven times a day will I bleſs Thy Name;
LORD JESUS.

Behold, all Creation praiſes Thy Holy Name;
LORD JESUS.

Dominion is Thine, & Power alſo is Thine;
LORD JESUS.

I will ſing unto Thee, my GOD, for that Thou haſt ſaved me;
LORD JESUS.

Every knee ſhall bow before Thee, of things in Heaven, & things in earth;
LORD JESUS.

Every tongue alſo ſhall confeſs Thy Holy Name;
LORD JESUS.

Turn away Thy Face from my ſins;
LORD JESUS.

For Thou, O GOD, haſt blotted out all my tranſgreſſions;
LORD JESUS.

Thou

Thou knoweſt all my thoughts, & Thou ſearcheſt my reins;
>   *LORD JESUS.*

O create a clean heart within me;
>   *LORD JESUS.*

Take not Thy HOLY SPIRIT from me;
>   *LORD JESUS.*

Incline Thine Ear unto me, & hear me ſpeedily;
>   *LORD JESUS.*

Lead me in the way of Thy Teſtimonies;
>   *LORD JESUS.*

Thy Kingdom, O my GOD, is an everlaſting Kingdom;
>   *LORD JESUS.*

Thou art the SON of GOD; I believe in Thee;
>   *LORD JESUS.*

O Thou, Who takeſt away the ſins of the world, have mercy on me;
>   *LORD JESUS.*

Forgive me the multitude of my offences;
>   *LORD JESUS.*

Every

Every living thing praises Thy Holy Name;
LORD JESUS.

Have, then, patience with me, & leave me not to perish;
LORD JESUS.

I will rise early to praise Thy Name;
LORD JESUS.

Thy yoke is easy, & Thy burden is light;
LORD JESUS.

Hear me in an acceptable time;
LORD JESUS.

Oh, how lovely is Thy Name, Thou Holy One;
LORD JESUS.

Keep me from all assaults of the devil;
LORD JESUS.

Shed abroad upon me the sweet fruit of Thy Truth;
LORD JESUS.

Give me Thy lasting Peace, & forgive me all my sins;
LORD JESUS.

I will

I will praise Thy Holy Name at all times in the Congregation;
LORD JESUS.

I will bless Thee, LORD JESUS; save me, & deliver me, for my hope is in Thee;
LORD JESUS.

And I will sing unto Thee a song of thanksgiving, as unto Thy FATHER, & the HOLY GHOST; for Thou hast redeemed me;
LORD JESUS.

A LITANY OF THE SAVIOUR OF THE WORLD.

[*Before Holy Communion.*]¹

Remember, O life-giving SAVIOUR, Thy Coming down from the Bosom of Thy FATHER to take our Nature of the Virgin Mary; &
Remember me.

Remember, O LORD of Mercies, how Thou didst hold intercourse with sinners such as I am; &
Remember me.

Remember, most Holy LORD, Thy Baptism in the river Jordan; &
Remember me.

Remember, O LORD, Who knowest all things,

---

¹ *From the Armenian.*

the taunts of the Pharisees, & the reproaches of the Scribes; &

Remember me.

Remember, O LORD, Who seest all things, from the beginning, Thy being betrayed by Judas, & the revilings of the High Priest; &

Remember me.

Remember, O powerful LORD, how they laid hands on Thee in Gethsemane, & how the soldiers did bind Thee captive; &

Remember me.

Remember, O LORD, Who canst do all things, how Thou didst stand before Caiaphas; & how Annas did question Thee; &

Remember me.

Remember, O LORD, ever long suffering, how the servants of the High Priest struck Thee with the palms of their hands; & how the furious multitude insulted Thee; &

Remember me.

Remember, O Thou patient SAVIOUR, how the

the Jews spat upon Thee, & beat Thee with a rod; &

Remember me.

Remember, O King of Kings, how Thou didst stand bound in Pilate's hall, & how Thou wast flogged by his order; &

Remember me.

Remember, O Thou Light unapproachable, the Robe of purple, & the Crown of thorns; &

Remember me.

Remember, O Lord, Who canst think no evil, that hour when Thou didst bear on Thy Shoulders the Cross that gives us life; &

Remember me.

Remember, O Thou Who art exalted on High, how they raised Thee on the Tree that gives us life, & how they fastened Thee to it with nails; &

Remember me.

Remember, O Lord, ah! do not forget Thy burning thirst, & Thy drink of vinegar & gall; &

Remember me.

Remem-

Remember, O LORD, Ah! do not forget Thy Cry of agony: My GOD, My GOD, why haſt Thou forſaken Me? &

Remember me.

Remember, that Wound in Thy Side inflicted by the cruel ſoldier; &

Remember me.

Remember, O LORD, Oh do not forget, the ſhedding of Thy Holy & precious BLOOD on the Croſs, & how Thou didſt bow Thy Divine Head; & in mercy

Remember me.

Remember, O Thou Who liveſt for ever, Thy being Buried three days; Thy Reſurrection as GOD, & LORD of Life; & Thy Aſcenſion in Majeſty; & in mercy

Remember me.

Remember, Oh! remember, Thou Who remembereſt all things, how Thou didſt ſuffer, & didſt bear all thoſe things for poor ſinners, of whom I am the chief; & in mercy

Remember me, moſt merciful LORD.

A LIT-

A LITANY OF THE LORD JESUS.

[*Before Holy Communion.*][1]

LORD JESUS, accept my prayer;
   O CHRIST, hear me.

O JESUS, Who sitteft on Thy Throne of Glory SAVIOUR of the world;
   Have mercy on me.

O JESUS, SON of GOD, & only Source of my joy;
   Have mercy on me.

O JESUS, Thou Good Shepherd, Who didft give Thy Life for the fheep, I befeech Thee;
   Have mercy on me.

O JESUS, Advocate with the FATHER, have mercy on me; &
   Intercede for me.

---
[1] *From an Ethiopic MS.*

O JESUS,

O Jesus, Thou Friend of sinners, full of Grace & Love, have mercy on me; &
Intercede for me.

O Jesus, Thou Gate of Heaven, have mercy on me; &
Intercede for me.

O Jesus, the Way of Life, have mercy on me; &
Intercede for me.

O Jesus, Thou Morning Star, shine bright in me; &
Intercede for me.

O Jesus, Thou Healer of all our infirmities, keep me; &
Intercede for me.

O Jesus, Thou only Refuge of sinners;
Intercede for me.

O Jesus, Who comfortest those that are of a broken heart;
Intercede for me.

O Jesus, Thou that art the help of Thy people, help me; &
Intercede for me.

O Jesus,

O Jesus, Thou Lamb of God, That takeſt away the ſins of the world;
Hear me, O Lord.

O Jesus, Thou Lamb of God, That takeſt away the ſins of the world;
Remit me my ſins, O Lord.

O Lord Jesu Christ, Son of God, Who loveſt ſinners, & Who takeſt away their ſins with Thy precious Blood, have mercy on me; &
Remit me my ſins, O Lord.

O Lord Jesus Christ, hear me; &
Have mercy on me.

O Lord Jesus Christ, Saviour of my Soul; I put all my truſt and confidence in Thee; hear me; &
Remit me my ſins, O Lord.

A LITANY OF THE LORD CHRIST.

[*An Eucharistic Prayer.*]¹

Help us, O GOD, our SAVIOUR ;

From the dominion of all vices ;
 Good LORD, deliver us.

From all blindness of heart ;
 Good LORD.

From all evil ;
 Good LORD.

We sinners ;
 Do beseech Thee to hear us.

That Thou give us a sure Hope ;
 We beseech Thee.

That Thou vouchsafe us a right Faith ;
 We.

---

¹ *From a Litany in Martene of the Tenth Century.*

That Thou beſtow on us perfect Love ;
We.

That Thou mortify in us the loathſome forms of all vices ;
We.

That Thou quicken us with the excellency of all Virtues ;
We.

That, by Thine Incarnation, Thou wouldeſt open for us an entrance into the Holy of Holies ;
We.

That, by this Moſt Holy Myſtery, Thou wouldeſt renew our Souls & bodies ;
We.

That, by It, Thou wouldeſt purify our conſciences ;
We.

That Thou wouldeſt not ſuffer this Tremendous Myſtery to become our condemnation ;
We.

That we may handle with pure hands this Ineffable Sacrament ;
We.

That

That we may receive It with pure minds;
We.

That, by It, we may obtain pardon of all sins;
We.

That, by It, we may be able evermore to cleave unto Thee;
We.

That, by It, we may be thought worthy to have Thee dwelling in us, & ourselves to dwell in Thee;
We.

That it may please Thee, to pour into our hearts the Grace of the HOLY SPIRIT;
We.

That it may please Thee, to preserve the Christian people who have been redeemed by Thy most precious BLOOD;
We.

That Thou vouchsafe us a place of repentance;
We.

A LITANY OF JESUS, THE INCARNATE GOD.

[*On the Mysteries of the Incarnation;*[1] *in thanksgiving for the H. Eucharist.*[2]]

JESUS, Incarnate GOD,
  Have mercy upon us.

JESUS, a Mediating Judge; an Avenging GOD become Loving; the Silent Word; & the Redeemer redeemed;
  Have mercy.

JESUS, a Shepherd become a Sheep; the Light in darkness; a Spirit become Flesh; an offended GOD become a SAVIOUR;
  Have mercy.

---

[1] *From Avrillon's Guide for passing Advent holily.*
[2] *From the Super Oblata, & Post Communion Prayers for the Season of Advent, in the Sacramentary of S. Gregory.*

JESUS,

OF JESUS, THE INCARNATE GOD.

Jesus, born of a Virgin Mother; the Blessed One in tears; Providence in want; & a Sovereign serving;
Have mercy.

Jesus, a loving Majesty; Greatness in lowliness; Immensity inclosed; & Almighty in weakness;
Have mercy.

Jesus, the Undying One subject to death; Glory in ignominy; Uncreated Wisdom become foolishness; Liberty in slavery; an Innocent Penitent;
Have mercy.

Jesus, Holiness laden with sins; Eternity made subject to time; a Priest the Victim; God a Babe;
Have mercy.

Jesus, God made Man;
Have mercy.

We sinners;
Do beseech Thee.

That Thou mercifully regard the Sacrifice offered

offered to Thee, that It may cleanse us from the defects of nature, and make us acceptable to Thy Name;
We beseech Thee.

That our Souls may obtain that which they long for; that they may be kindled by Thy SPIRIT; & that like lamps, replenished with the Divine Gift, we may shine as bright lights in Thy Presence;
We beseech Thee.

That, by the participation of this Sacred Mystery, what we believe, & look for, we may, expecting, receive;
We beseech Thee.

That Thou be propitious to the prayers & Sacrifices of our lowliness; that we, who have no merits to plead, may be succoured by the protection of Thy Mercy;
We beseech Thee.

That, being filled with the Food of Spiritual Nourishment, Thou wouldest teach us to despise earthly things, & to love the Heavenly;
We beseech Thee.

That

That the Sacrifice of our Devotions being offered unto Thee, It may both accomplish the Sacred Mystery ordained to us, & work in us marvellously, Thy Salvation;
We beseech Thee.

That, by Thy Clemency, these Divine Supplies may prepare us, cleansed from all sin, for Thy everlasting Kingdom;
We beseech Thee.

That the Gifts be well pleasing unto Thee, wherewith we have celebrated the Mysteries of our deliverance, & our life;
We beseech Thee.

That Thy Grace may preserve us, & bestow upon us everlasting Life;
We beseech Thee.

That the Fruits of our Devotion which we have offered, may correspond to the Gifts which Thou hast consecrated;
We beseech Thee.

That, having sanctified the Offerings of Thy Church, we may, through these Venerable Mysteries,

teries, be worthy to be refreshed with Bread from Heaven;
We beseech Thee.

That the All Holy Mysteries which Thou hast bestowed, both guard our restoration, & be to us a Remedy here, & for ever;
We beseech Thee.

That we who are replenished with the Virtues of the Heavenly Table, may both long for what is right, & receive what we long for;
We beseech Thee.

That we may have new Life in Him, through Whose Heavenly Mystery we have the True Meat, & True Drink;
We beseech Thee.

That, through this All Holy Communion, we may be found in His Form, in Whom our substance is with the FATHER;
We beseech Thee.

That we, who rejoice in Thy Holy Sacrifice, may, by meet conversation, be found worthy to belong to Thy Holy Fellowship;
We beseech Thee.

That,

That, as He Who was born a Man, the Same shone upon us as GOD; so, may this Earthly Substance have bestowed upon us That which is Divine;
We beseech Thee.

That He Who is the Author of our Divine birth, may also be the Giver of our Immortality;
We beseech Thee.

LITANIES

LITANIES OF EMMANUEL, GOD WITH US.

[*On the Incarnation of our Blessed* LORD.][1]

I.

EMMANUEL,

Who wast looked for by the ancient Fathers, announced by an Angel, conceived by a Virgin, & in the end of the world, wast given unto men;

Be clement.

Whose Incarnation wrought the Salvation of the world, & Whose Passion procured the Redemption of Man whom Thou hast created;

Be clement.

Who art without end, & without number;

Be clement.

Who not only remittest sins, but also justifiest the sinners; & Who not only forgivest the guilty, but bestowest on them gifts & rewards;

Be clement.

---

[1] *From the Prayers for Advent, in the Sacramentary of S. Gregory.*

Whose Forerunner, in his birth, in his preaching, & in the wilderness, was S. John the Baptist;
Be clement.

Who hast restored us by the Grace of Thy first Coming; & hast promised the Kingdom in Thy Second;
Be clement.

Whom the Unbegotten Greatness of the FATHER's Majesty begat, ever the SON, begotten before all times;
Be clement.

Who, by Thy Incarnation, didst chase away the darkness of the world; &, by Thy glorious Nativity, didst cast bright beams upon Creation;
Be clement.

Who willedst that Thy all-holy Nativity should be announced by Angels unto shepherds;
Be clement.

Who, by Thy Incarnation, Invisible in Thy Substance, through Flesh, appearedst visible in ours, didst join things earthly to Heavenly;
Be clement.

Who,

Who, by the Mystery of Thy Incarnation, didst cause the new Light of Thy Brightness to shine upon the eyes of our mind;
Be clement.

We sinners, beseech Thee;
To hear us, O LORD GOD.

That we so celebrate the Mysteries of Thy first Advent, that we may await the second without fear;
Grant us, Gracious LORD.

That Thou defend us from all adversity in this mortal life, & show Thyself appeased in the Day of Judgment;
Grant us.

That Thou wash out from us, all which in the future sifting Thou wouldest punish; that then, Thou mayest find nothing to condemn;
Grant us.

That Thou supply us with aids for this life present, & impart to us the rewards of everlasting Bliss;
Grant us.

That

That we, who are weighed down under the yoke of sin, through the servitude of the old man, may be set free by the Mystery of Thy new Birth;

Grant us.

That, by Thy Gift, we may be found worthy to be humble amid things prosperous; & in adversity, free from care;

Grant us.

That no earthly words or actions may hinder us from hastening to meet Thee; but that the instruction of Heavenly Wisdom may make us partakers of Thyself;

Grant us.

That Thou gird up the loins of our minds with Thy Divine Virtue, that we may be found meet to receive the prize of Heavenly Dignities;

Grant us.

That, by the Mystery of Thy Nativity, the minds of believers may be prepared, & the hearts of unbelievers may be subdued;

Grant us.

That the celebration of Thy Incarnation may ever reſtore us, Whoſe new & wondrous Birth removed man's decrepitude ;
Grant us.

That they who have been redeemed by Thy Grace, may, through Thy Adoption, be freed from fear ;
Grant us.

That what we long earneſtly to celebrate, in time, we may, without end, enjoy;
Grant us.

II.

Emmanuel,
Who, Only-Begotten, & Co-Eternal with the Father, waſt born of a Virgin Mother, in real Subſtance of our Fleſh ;
Be clement.

Who, by the Myſtery of Thy Incarnation, favedſt us from the impending peril of our ſins ; & madeſt us meet to obtain Reſcue through Thy protection, & Salvation through Thy deliverance ;
Be clement.

Whoſe

OF EMMANUEL, GOD WITH US.

Whose promised Coming is both believed in the past, in the Incarnation; & is looked for in the future, in Judgment;
Be clement.

Who hast appointed that the beginning, & perfection of all Religion, should be in the Mystery of Thy Nativity;
Be clement.

Who, by Thy first Coming, Thy true Light made all things clear & manifest, both in understanding, & to sight;
Be clement.

Who dost gladden us with the annual expectation of our Redemption;
Be clement.

Who didst wonderfully form, & still more wonderfully reform the dignity of man's nature in Thy Nativity;
Be clement.

Who, by Thy Birth of the B. Virgin, hast made us to be free from all injury from our first father;
Be clement.

Who,

Who, by Thy unspeakable Gift, didst provide that our human nature, created in Thy Likeness, but made unlike through sin, should not perish by everlasting damnation;
Be clement.

Who, by Thy Infinite Mercy, didst thence restore life, whence sin had brought in death;
Be clement.

Who, by Thy wondrous Incarnation, hast effaced the transgression of the Virgin of old, by a new & undefiled Virgin, Mary;
Be clement.

Who, by the wonderful Sacrament of Thy Advent, hast made it known that what was promised by the holy Prophets, hath been fulfilled;
Be clement.

We sinners;
Do beseech Thee to hear us.

That we who rejoice in Thy first Coming, may, at Thy second Coming, receive the reward of everlasting Life;
Grant us, Gracious LORD.

That,

That, free from all defilements of ſin, we may await without terror the Day of tremendous trial;
Grant us.

That, through Thy Coming, we may both know Thee with our whole mind; & follow with our whole heart, what is pleaſing unto Thee;
Grant us.

That Thou lead us to everlaſting Rewards, Who redeemedſt us from darkneſs; that Thou juſtify us, Who haſt redeemed us; & that Thy Exaltation may defend us from evil, Whoſe Lowlineſs raiſed us to life;
Grant us.

That thoſe who truſt in Thy loving Mercy, may ſpeedily be freed from all adverſity;
Grant us.

That Thou come to our relief, that from all the perils which hang over us for our ſins, we may find Grace to be ſaved;
Grant us.

That

That we may rejoice together in the Unity of the Faith, that hereafter we may meet Thee undefiled in the Company of Thy Saints;
Grant us.

That Thy Nativity in the Flesh may free us, Whom the servitude of the old man holdeth, under the yoke of sin;
Grant us.

That we, who have received this New Creation, may be stripped of all contagion with the old decrepitude;
Grant us.

That we may be numbered in Thy Inheritance, in Whom the sum of all men's Salvation consists;
Grant us.

That Thou grant us gloriously to believe in, & with praise to confess, Thee, made Man for the redemption of our Souls;
Grant us.

A LIT-

A LITANY OF CHRIST, PRESENT IN THE MOST HOLY SACRAMENT.

[*An Eucharistic Prayer.*]¹

O CHRIST, the Everlasting Truth, the Maker of the world, the Maker of the Law, & the Giver of life;
Be merciful.

O CHRIST, our GOD, Saint of Saints, Creator of men, & the LORD of the Angels;
Be merciful.

O CHRIST, our Sanctification & Redemption, the Consolation of pilgrims, the Eternal Shepherd, & the Everlasting Fruition of Saints;
Be merciful.

O CHRIST, Healer of the Sick, Fountain of life, King of Heaven, & tender Comforter;
Be merciful.

---

¹ *From the Fourth Book of the Imitation of* CHRIST.

O Christ, our Inexhaustible Support, & sweet Refection of the Soul, our Guest, Companion, Friend, & Spouse;
Be merciful.

O Christ, the Protector of the Soul, the Restorer of human weakness, & the Giver of all inward consolation;
Be merciful.

O Christ, the Fountain of Grace & Divine Mercy, the Fountain of Goodness & all Purity, Sovereign Remedy, everlasting Love, our whole Good, & Happiness Which has no limit;
Be merciful.

We sinners;
Beseech Thee.

That, in this Holy Sacrament, Spiritual Grace may be conferred; Virtue, which was lost, may be restored; & Beauty, which had been disfigured, be returned;
O CHRIST, hear us.

That, out of the fulness of Devotion here given,

given, not the Mind only, but the body alſo, may feel an increaſe of ſtrength;

O CHRIST, bear us.

That, in ſimplicity of Heart, with firm Faith, & at Thy Commandment, we may draw near unto Thee with hope & reverence;

O CHRIST, bear us.

That we may be diſſolved, & overflow with love toward Thee; & never ſuffer any conſolation to enter in, which comes not from Thee;

O CHRIST, bear us.

That this Precious Sacrament may be the Medicine of Spiritual languor; & that by It, our vices may be cured, our paſſions bridled, & our temptations overcome, or weakened;

O CHRIST, bear us.

That, by theſe Holy Myſteries, Grace may be infuſed, Virtue may be increaſed, Faith be confirmed, Hope ſtrengthened, & Love inflamed;

O CHRIST, bear us.

That we, who of ourſelves are cold, hard, & indevout,

indevout, may by Thee be enabled to become devout, cheerful, & fervent;

O Christ, hear us.

That, with full resignation, & entire will, we may offer up ourselves on the Altar of our hearts, to the honour of Thy Name;

O Christ, hear us.

That, by the Blessed Eucharist, we may be healed of our sins & passions; & may obtain to be made more strong & vigilant against the deceits of the devil;

O Christ, hear us.

That we may be preserved from over-fearfulness, & perplexity, from the crafty & fanciful suggestions of Satan, from over-great solicitude, & from such anxiety & scrupulousness as would hinder us from Holy Communion;

O Christ, hear us.

That we, coming unto Thee, may be sanctified by Thee, & united to Thee; that we may receive new Grace, & be stirred up to amendment of life;

O Christ, hear us.

That

That we, by means of Sacred Communion, may withdraw our Hearts from all created things, & may learn, more & more, to relish things Heavenly & Eternal;

O Christ, hear us.

That, in these Holy Mysteries, we may seek the Grace of Devotion earnestly, may ask it fervently, & may wait for it, with patience & confidence;

O Christ, hear us.

That we may receive this Heavenly Visitation with gratefulness; may keep it humbly; may work with it diligently; & commit the term, & manner of it, unto Thee;

O Christ, hear us.

That Thou mayest refresh Thy hungry suppliants; inflame our coldness with Thy Love; & enlighten our blindness with the brightness of Thy Presence;

O Christ, hear us.

That Thou be pleased, for us, to turn all earthly things into bitterness; all things grievous,
into

into occasions for patience; & all low & created things, into contempt & oblivion;

   O Christ, hear us.

That Thou wouldst wholly inflame, consume, & transform us into Thyself, that we may be made one Spirit with Thee, by the Grace of inward Union, & the meltings of ardent Love;

   O Christ, hear us.

A LITANY OF THE LORD JESUS.

[*Present in the Blessed Sacrament.*]¹

Lord Jesus,
Living Bread that camest down from Heaven;
Have mercy upon us.

Hidden God, & Saviour;
Have.

Corn of the Elect;
Have.

Wine, Whose fruit are Virgins;
Have.

Bread of Fatness, & Royal Dainties;
Have.

Perpetual Sacrifice;
Have.

Pure Oblation;
Have.

---

¹ *From an ancient Litany, of Flemish origin?*

Lamb without Spot ;
Have.

Moſt pure Feaſt ;
Have.

Food of Angels ;
Have.

Hidden Manna ;
Have.

Memorial of the Wonder of GOD ;
Have.

Word made Fleſh, dwelling in us ;
Have.

Sacred Victim ;
Have.

Chalice of Benediction ;
Have.

Moſt High, & Adorable Sacrament ;
Have.

Moſt Holy of all Sacrifices ;
Have.

True Propitiation for the living, & the dead ;
Have.

Heavenly

Heavenly Antidote againſt the poiſon of ſin ;
Have.

Moſt Wonderful of all Miracles ;
Have.

Moſt Holy Commemoration of the Paſſion of Christ ;
Have.

Gift tranſcending all fulneſs ;
Have.

Special memorial of Divine Love ;
Have.

Richneſs of Divine Bounty ;
Have.

Moſt Auguſt & Holy Myſtery ;
Have.

Medicine of Immortality ;
Have.

Tremendous, & Life-giving Sacrament ;
Have.

Bread made Fleſh, by the Omnipotence of the Word ;
Have.

Unbloody

Unbloody Sacrifice ;
Have.

Our Feaſt, at once, & our Fellow Gueſt ;
Have.

Sweeteſt Banquet, at which Angels miniſter ;
Have.

Sacrament of Piety ;
Have.

Bond of Charity ;
Have.

Prieſt, & Victim ;
Have.

Spiritual Sweetneſs, taſted in its proper Source;
Have.

Refreſhment of Holy Souls ;
Have.

Nouriſhment of ſuch as die in the LORD ;
Have.

Pledge of future Glory ;
Have.

Be merciful ;
Spare us, Good LORD.

Be merciful;
Graciously hear us, Good LORD.

From an unworthy reception of Thy BODY, & BLOOD;
Good LORD, *deliver us.*

From the luft of the flefh;
Good LORD.

From the luft of the eyes;
Good LORD.

From the pride of life;
Good LORD.

Through the defire, wherewith Thou didft defire to eat this Paffover with Thy Difciples;
Good LORD.

Through that profound Humility, wherewith Thou didft wafh their feet;
Good LORD.

Through that ardent Charity, wherewith Thou didft inftitute this Divine Sacrament;
Good LORD.

Through Thy moft precious BLOOD, which Thou haft left us on Thy Altar;
Good LORD.

Through the Five Wounds of Thy most Holy Body, which Thou didst receive for us;
Good LORD.

We sinners;
Do beseech Thee to hear us.

That Thou wouldest vouchsafe,
To preserve, & increase our Faith, reverence, & devotion, towards this Adorable Sacrament;
We beseech Thee, hear us.

To conduct us, through a true confession of our sins, to a frequent reception of the most Holy Eucharist;
We.

To deliver us from all heresy, perfidy, & blindness of heart;
We.

To impart to us the precious, & Heavenly Fruits of this Holy Sacrifice;
We.

To strengthen, & defend us, at the hour of death, by this Heavenly Nourishment;
We.

A LITANY OF THE LORD JESU CHRIST.

[*An Eucharistic Prayer.*][1]

JESU, Most Sweet SAVIOUR, Who hast prepared a Table before us, against them that trouble us;
Have mercy upon us.

JESU, Most Worthy of all Love, Who hast said—Come unto Me, all ye that labour, & are heavy laden, & I will refresh you;
Have mercy upon us.

JESU, Most Pitiful, Who hadst compassion on the multitude, & didst feed them with Bread in the wilderness;
Have mercy upon us.

JESU, Most Bountiful, Who hast given unto us the True Bread that yieldeth Royal Dainties;
Have mercy upon us.

---

[1] *From the Paradise of the Christian Soul.*

Jesu, Most Benign, Who hast said—My **Flesh** is Meat indeed, & My **Blood** is Drink indeed;
Have mercy upon us.

Jesu, Most Sweet, Whom the Centurion did not think himself worthy to receive under his roof;
Have mercy upon us.

Jesu, Most Lowly, Who didst declare—They that are whole need not a Physician, but they that are sick;
Have mercy upon us.

Jesu, Great & Marvellous King, Who hast prepared for us a great Feast, & hast deigned to invite us to it;
Have mercy upon us.

Jesu, Most Loving, Who didst desire to eat this Passover with Thy Disciples, before Thy Passion;
Have mercy upon us.

Jesu, Most Pure, Who didst wash Thy Apostles' feet, when about to institute the Holy Sacrament;
Have mercy upon us.

Jesu,

Jesu, Most Tender, Who didst leave us a lasting Monument of Thy Love in the Sacrifice of the Altar;
Have mercy upon us.

Jesu, Most Truthful, Who giving Thyself to be Meat & Drink, didst say—This is My BODY & This is My BLOOD;
Have mercy upon us.

Jesu, Most Thankful, Who, when this Mystery was accomplished, didst give thanks unto Thy FATHER;
Have mercy upon us.

Jesu, Priest for ever, Who didst offer Thyself, as a Victim, upon the Altar of the Cross;
Have mercy upon us.

Jesu, Most Compassionate, Who didst join Thyself to the Disciples on the Emmaus Road, & didst make Thyself known to them in the Breaking of BREAD;
Have mercy upon us.

We sinners, do beseech Thee;
To hear us, O LORD GOD.

That our enemies may never prevail against us,

us, that we may fear no evil, becaufe Thou art with us, & in this Holy Sacrament, art moft inwardly prefent to us;

Hear us, Good LORD; hear us, Good LORD, we humbly befeech Thee.

That we may be delivered from the weight of thofe fins, which are like a fore burden, too heavy for us to bear;

Hear us, Good LORD.

That our Soul may be fatisfied, even as it were with marrow & fatnefs; & that our Heart may not be fmitten down & withered, fo that we forget to eat our Bread;

Hear us, Good LORD.

That we may fo worthily eat this Bread, & drink this Cup, that we hunger no more, nor thirft any more, nor die eternally;

Hear us, Good LORD.

That we may come to this Divine Feaft with joy & alacrity, yet never without being clothed in a wedding garment;

Hear us, Good LORD.

That, as the Hart panteth after the water brooks,

brooks, even so, our Soul may pant after Thee, O GOD;
Hear us, Good LORD.

That, in this Holy Sacrament, Thou mayest wash us throughly from our wickedness, & cleanse us from our sin;
Hear us, Good LORD.

That we may gather the Fruit of Life & Immortality; & that by It our youth may be renewed as an Eagle's;
Hear us, Good LORD.

That for these so great benefits our Soul, & all that is within us, may bless Thy Holy Name;
Hear us, Good LORD.

That we stagger not in unbelief, at the Words of Thy Lips, for Thou art Faithful Who hast promised;
Hear us, Good LORD.

That we may be always mindful of Thee, & may constantly adore Thy Power, Wisdom, & Goodness;
Hear us, Good LORD.

That

That we may never retire from this Surpassing Feast with a thankless heart; but that our Soul may more & more burn with love towards Thee;
Hear us, Good LORD.

That as we believe Thee truly present under these Visible Forms, so we may at length be counted worthy to behold Thee with unveiled Face;
Hear us, Good LORD.

A LITANY OF OUR BLESSED LORD.

[*In thanksgiving for Holy Communion.*][1]

We sinners, do beseech Thee;
To hear us, O LORD GOD.

And that it may please Thee, to grant, that through this Spiritual Food, fellowship with the HOLY GHOST may be received & taken; so that, by this Heavenly Nourishment, we may be transformed into the Very Flesh of Him, Who by His Incarnation adopted ours;
Grant us, Gracious LORD.

That Thou grant us a Communion unto Faith, without shame; Love without dissimulation; & a cheerful performance of Thy Will;
Grant us, Gracious LORD.

That Thou bestow on us alacrity for every

---

[1] *Chiefly from early English Sources.*

Spiritual

Spiritual Gift; hindrance from all adversity; strength, in all dangers; & patience in all sufferings;

Grant us, Gracious LORD.

That it may please Thee, to guard our Soul, to stablish our body; to elevate our senses; & to direct our conversation;

Grant us, Gracious LORD.

That it may please Thee, to bless our actions; to fulfil our prayers; to inspire holy thoughts; to pardon the past; to correct the future; & to bring us, by this Blessed Mystery, to the Kingdom of Heaven;

Grant us, Gracious LORD.

That Thou heal the palate of our heart, that we may taste the sweetness of Thy Love; & that Thou cleanse it of all infirmities, that we may find sweetness in nothing out of Thee;

Grant us, Gracious LORD.

That the true perception of Thy BODY & BLOOD may not be unto us for our judgment to condemnation; but may be the desired remission of all our sins, both of Soul & body;

Grant us, Gracious LORD.

That

That the Most Blessed Eucharist may become the gracious & mighty governance of our Souls & bodies; & our admission into Life, both present, & everlasting;

Grant us, Gracious LORD.

That Thy Holy Communion, may through Thy Grace & Pity, be fragrance to our Soul; salvation & sanctity in every temptation; & peace & joy in all tribulation;

Grant us, Gracious LORD.

That, to us, It may become Light & Strength in every word & work; our comfort & defence to the end; & at our death, for our deliverance, & the destruction of the snares of all our enemies, visible & invisible;

Grant us, Gracious LORD.

That Thy Holy BODY & Thy Precious BLOOD may be to us an armour of Faith, & a shield of good purpose; a riddance of all vices; & an extermination of all evil desires, & concupiscence;

Grant us, Gracious LORD.

That It be, to us, an increase of love & patience, of humility & obedience, & of all virtues; a pera perfect quieting of all our impulses, fleshly & spiritual; a firm adherence to Thee, the One True GOD: & a blessed consummation of our end;

Grant us, Gracious LORD.

That whatever we have done amiss, at Thy Holy Altar, in sinful, unlawful, or unclean thoughts; in too little reverence; in any unworthy gesture, act, or neglect; in vain repetition of words, or distraction of thought, or in any other manner whatever, Thou mayest mercifully pardon;

Grant us, Gracious LORD.

That these Sacramental Mysteries may extirpate, in us, the pestilence of pride, the lust of gluttony, & the petulance of speech; & that They may be, unto us, consolation in affliction; love & exceeding delight in every good purpose; patience in tribulation & anguish; medicine in sickness; & finally, consolation & defence in the hour of death;

Grant us, Gracious LORD.

A LITANY OF JESUS, GOD & MAN.

[*In preparation for the Most Holy Communion.*][1]

JESUS, GOD, & Man,
In Two Natures & One Divine Person;
> *LORD, I am not worthy that Thou shouldest come under my roof; but speak the word only, & Thy servant shall be healed.*

Our Wonderful GOD, Who dost vouchsafe to be present upon the Altar when the Priest pronounces the words of Consecration;
> *LORD, I am not worthy.*

Our Incomprehensible GOD, Who, though the Heaven of Heavens cannot contain Thee, art pleased to dwell among men;
> *LORD, I am not worthy.*

---

[1] *From an old Litany of German origin.*

Our Sovereign King, Who, though Thy Throne is attended by glorified Spirits, yet doſt not decline the ſervice of men;
LORD, I am not worthy.

Our Heavenly Phyſician, Who vouchſafeſt to deſcend, from Thy Palace of Immortal Bliſs, to our houſes of clay, to viſit us on beds of ſickneſs, & to give Thyſelf to comfort our ſorrows;
LORD, I am not worthy.

Our Glorious GOD, Who ſitteſt at the Right Hand of Thy Eternal FATHER, adored by innumerable Angels, & encompaſſed with the ſplendours of inacceſſible Light;
LORD, I am not worthy.

Our Gracious GOD, Who, condeſcending to the weakneſs of our nature, doſt cover Thy Glory under the familiar Forms of Bread & Wine; & ſo, doſt give Thyſelf to us miſerable ſinners;
LORD, I am not worthy.

Our Merciful GOD, Who, concealing the Brightneſs of Thy Majeſty under theſe low & humble Veils, doſt invite us to approach unto Thee,

Thee, to lay open our miseries before Thy Eyes, & to deliver our petitions into Thy Hands;
LORD, I am not worthy.

Our Pitiful GOD, Who, to communicate Thy Divine Nature to sinners, dost humble Thyself to descend into our hearts, & by an inconceivable Union to become One with us;
LORD, I am not worthy.

Have mercy;
Hear us, Good LORD.

Have mercy;
Spare us, Good LORD.

JESUS, GOD, & Man;
The Bread of Life, Which came down from Heaven; of Which, whosoever eats, shall live for ever;
Grant that I may go to the Altar of GOD, & receive the Cup of Salvation.

The Heavenly Manna, Whose Sweetness nourishes Thy Elect in the desert of this world;
Grant that I may go.

The Food of Angels, Whoſe ſweetneſs fills our hearts with Celeſtial Joys;
Grant that I may go.

The Lamb without ſpot, Who art daily ſacrificed, yet always remaineſt Alive; Who art continually conſumed, yet ſtill remaineſt Perfect;
Grant that I may go.

The Good Shepherd, Who layeſt down Thy Life for Thy ſheep, & feedeſt them with Thine Own Body;
Grant that I may go.

Who, in this Auguſt & Venerable Myſtery, art Thyſelf both Prieſt & Victim;
Grant that I may go.

Who, in the Sacred Memorial of Thy Death, haſt conſummated all Thy Wonders into One Stupendous Miracle;
Grant that I may go.

Who, in this Adorable Sacrament, haſt contracted all Thy Bleſſings into One Ineſtimable Bounty;
Grant that I may go.

Who,

Who, by this blessed Fruit of the Tree of Life, dost restore us again to Immortality;
Grant that I may go.

Who, by becoming Thyself our daily Food, in this life, dost prepare us to feed on Thee eternally, in the next;
Grant that I may go.

Who, in this Divine Banquet, givest us possession of Thy Grace here, & a certain pledge of our glory hereafter;
Grant that I may go.

Spare us, Good LORD;
& pardon our sins.

Spare us, Good LORD;
& hear our prayers.

From presuming to measure the depth of Divine Omnipotence by the short line of human reason;
Good LORD, deliver us.

From all distraction & irreverence, in assisting at this Awful Sacrifice;
Good LORD.

From neglecting to approach Thy Holy Table; & from coming to It unprepared;
Good LORD.

From an unworthy, & fruitless reception of this Adorable Sacrament;
Good LORD.

From all hardness of heart, & ingratitude for so unspeakable a Blessing;
Good LORD.

By Thy irresistible Power, which changeth the course of nature as Thou willest;
Be favourable, O CHRIST.

By Thy unsearchable Wisdom, which disposeth all things in perfect order;
Be favourable.

By Thy Infinite Goodness, which freely bestows Thyself, in this Incomprehensible Mystery;
Be favourable.

By Thy most Sacred BODY, broken, for us, upon the Cross, & really given unto us, in the Holy Communion;
Be favourable.

By

By Thy moſt Precious BLOOD, poured out, for us, upon the Croſs, & really given unto us in the Cup of Bleſſing;
Be favourable.

We ſinners, moſt humbly beſeech Thee;
To bear us, O LORD JESU CHRIST.

And that it may pleaſe Thee to grant
That we may always believe nothing more reaſonable, than to ſubmit our reaſon unto Thee;
We beſeech Thee to bear us, Good LORD.

That, by this Sacred Oblation, we may acknowledge Thine infinite Perfections in Thyſelf, & Thy ſupreme Dominion over all things;
We beſeech Thee.

That, by this Adorable Sacrifice, we may acknowledge our perpetual dependence upon Thee, & our abſolute ſubjection to Thy Will;
We beſeech Thee.

That we may eternally magnify Thy Goodneſs, Who, having no need of us, haſt contrived ſuch endearing motives to make us love Thee;
We beſeech Thee.

That

That we may thankfully comply with Thy Gracious Defire of being united to us, by a fervent defire to be made One with Thee;
We befeech Thee.

That, before we approach the Banquet of Divine Love, we may endeavour to be reconciled to Thee, & be in perfect charity with all the world;
We befeech Thee.

That, at the moment of receiving Thy Sacred Body & Thy Precious Blood our Souls may be diffolved in reverence & love, to attend on & entertain fo glorious a Gueft;
We befeech Thee.

That, returning from the Holy Euchariſt, we may collect all our thoughts to praife & blefs Thee, & endeavour to effect the amendment of our lives;
We befeech Thee.

That, by this Heavenly Prefervative, our heart may be healed of all infirmities, & our will ſtrengthened againſt all relapfes;
We befeech Thee.

That,

That, as by Faith, we adore Thee here, prefent beneath thefe Sacred Veils; fo, we may hereafter behold Thee Face to face, & eternally rejoice in the Beatific Vifion;

We befeech Thee.

CONCLUSIONS.

LORD, have mercy upon us.
CHRIST, have mercy upon us.
LORD, have mercy upon us.

Let us pray.
Our FATHER:
& lead us not into temptation;
But deliver us from evil.   Amen.

[*Before Holy Communion.*]

I said, LORD, have mercy upon me;
Heal my soul, for I have sinned against Thee.

Turn Thee, O LORD, at the last;
& be gracious unto Thy servants.

Let Thy Mercy, O LORD, be upon us;
As our Hope is in Thee.

Let Thy Priests be clothed with Righteousness;
& let Thy saints sing with joyfulness.

Cleanse

Cleanse Thou me, O LORD, from my secret faults;
> *Keep Thy servant also from presumptuous sin.*

LORD, hear our prayer;
> *& let our cry come unto Thee.*

[*After Holy Communion.*]

Let all Thy Works praise Thee, O LORD;
> *& Thy Saints give thanks unto Thee.*

Thy Saints shall exult in Glory;
> *They shall rejoice in their beds.*

Not unto us, O LORD, not unto us;
> *But unto Thy Name, give Glory.*

LORD, hear our prayer;
> *& let our cry come unto Thee.*

VERSICLES AND RESPONSES FOR DIFFERENT SEASONS.[1]

[*For Advent, & Christmastide.*]

Raise up Thy Power, & come among us;
> *& save us.*

---

[1] *From the Paris Missal.*

Let Thy loving Mercy come also unto me, O LORD;
Even Thy Salvation, according unto Thy Word.

This GOD is our GOD for ever;
He shall be our Guide unto death.

Behold, GOD is my Helper;
The LORD is with them that uphold my soul.

Behold, Thou hast loved Truth;
The uncertain & hidden things Thou hast made manifest.

We will rejoice in Thy Salvation;
& triumph in the Name of the LORD our GOD.

[From the Epiphany to Quinquagesima.]

His Righteousness hath He openly showed in the sight of the Heathen;
He hath remembered His Mercy & Truth.

My SAVIOUR, Thou savest me from violence;
So shall I be saved from my enemies.

Show

Show Thy Servant the Light of Thy Countenance;
    & save me, for Thy Mercy's sake.

Lighten mine eyes, O LORD, that I sleep not in death;
    Lest mine enemy say, I have prevailed against him.

[*In Lent.*]

Turn us again, O LORD GOD of Hosts;
    Show the Light of Thy Countenance, & we shall be whole.

Arise, O LORD, & help us;
    & deliver us for Thy Mercy's sake.

O LORD, hear our prayer;
    & let our cry come unto Thee.

Our eyes wait upon the LORD our GOD;
    Until He have mercy upon us.

Hear my prayer, O LORD, & with Thine ears consider my calling;
    Hold not Thy Peace at my tears.

O deliver me from the wicked doers;
    & save me from the bloodthirsty men.

Out of the mouths of babes & sucklings;
Hast Thou perfected praise, O LORD.

CHRIST loved us, & hath given Himself for us;
An Offering, & a Sacrifice to GOD, *for a sweet smelling Savour.*

[*During Easter-Tide.*]

Thou hast made known unto me, O LORD, the ways of Life;
Thou shalt make me full of joy with Thy Countenance.

My Soul is athirst for GOD, yea, even for the living GOD;
When shall I come to appear before the Presence of GOD?

The LORD liveth, & blessed be my Strong Helper;
& praised be the GOD *of my Salvation.*

The LORD hath prepared His Seat in Heaven;
& His Kingdom ruleth over all.

Thou art the GOD that doeth wonders;
& hast declared Thy Power among the People.

Blessed

Bleſſed be the Name of the LORD;
> From this time forth, for evermore.

[*For the Seaſon after Trinity.*]

O give me the comfort of Thy Help again;
> *& ſtabliſh me with Thy Free Spirit.*

He gave them Bread from Heaven;
> *& man did eat Angels' Food.*

The LORD is high above all Heathen;
> *& His Glory above the Heaven.*

My Heart hath talked of Thee; Seek ye My Face;
> *Thy Face, O LORD, will I ſeek.*

Thou haſt been my Succour, O leave me not;
> *Neither forſake me, O GOD of my Salvation.*

Come ye to Him, & be enlightened;
> *& your faces ſhall not be confounded.*

My Hope hath been in Thee, O LORD;
> *My time is in Thy Hand.*

I will always give thanks unto the LORD;
> *His Praiſe ſhall ever be in my mouth.*

They

They that know Thy Name will put their truſt in Thee;
> *For Thou haſt never failed them that ſeek Thee.*

Our eyes wait upon the Lᴏʀᴅ our Gᴏᴅ;
> *Until He have mercy upon us.*

Teach me, O Lᴏʀᴅ, the Way of Thy Statutes;
> *& I ſhall keep it unto the end.*

Unto Thee, O Lᴏʀᴅ, will I lift up my Soul;
> *My Gᴏᴅ, I have put my truſt in Thee; O let me not be confounded.*

O ſend out Thy Light, & Thy Truth;
> *That they may lead me, & bring me unto Thy holy Hill.*

[*On the Feſtival of a Saint.*]

He gave them to glory in His marvellous Acts for ever;
> *That they might declare His Works with underſtanding.*

Behold,

Behold, GOD is my Helper;
The LORD is with them that uphold my Soul.

Behold, Thou haſt loved Truth;
The uncertain, & hidden things haſt Thou made manifeſt.

Bring preſents, & come into His Courts;
O worſhip the LORD in the beauty of Holineſs.

The LORD remembered us when we were in trouble;
& hath delivered us from our enemies.

Our fathers have declared unto us;
The noble Works that Thou didſt in their days.

Unto Thee, O LORD, do we give thanks;
Yea, unto Thee do we give thanks.

My mouth ſhall daily ſpeak of Thy Righteouſneſs & Salvation;
For I know no end thereof.

Thou ſhalt feed Thy People Iſrael;
& Thou ſhalt be a Captain over Iſrael.

Praiſe

Praise the Lord, all ye Angels of His;
Praise Him, all His Host.

Let the Saints be joyful with Glory;
Let them rejoice in their beds.

Glory be to the Father.
As it was in the beginning.

PRINTED BY JOSEPH MASTERS AND CO., ALDERSGATE STREET.

Preparing for Publication, Part II., containing

PENITENTIAL LITANIES,

BY THE SAME EDITOR.

www.ingramcontent.com/pod-product-compliance
Lightning Source LLC
Chambersburg PA
CBHW032152160426
43197CB00008B/883